COACHING PERSPECTIVES III

Center for Coaching Certification

Cathy Liska

Rebecca Cooley

Penny Ducharme

Ava Webb

Donna Leake

Wendy Glantz

Gina Wilson

Brian Beatty

Charlie Kiss

Jennifer Connell

Maria Van Parys

Nozomi Morgan

Jina Fernandez

Copyright © 2013 by the Center for Coaching Certification LLC

All rights reserved. No part of this publication may be reproduced, distributed, or transmitted in any form or by any means, including photocopying, recording, or other electronic or mechanical methods without the prior written permission of the publisher, except in the case of brief quotations embodied in critical reviews and certain other noncommercial uses permitted by copyright law. For permission requests, write to 5072 Coral Reef Drive, Johns Island, SC 29455.

Full rights to the individual chapters in this book are granted to the respective author for their use, and they may grant rights to their individual chapters as they deem appropriate.

Names and identifying details have been changed to protect the privacy of individuals.

The authors and publisher have made every effort to ensure accuracy and completeness of the information in this book. We assume no responsibility for errors, inaccuracies, omissions, or any inconsistencies herein. Any slights of people, places, or organizations are unintentional. Although the authors and publisher have made every effort to ensure that the information in this book was correct at press time, the authors and publisher do not assume and hereby disclaim any liability to any party for any loss, damage, or disruption, either direct or indirect, caused by errors or omissions, whether such errors or omissions result from negligence, accident, or any other cause.

The information in this book is meant to supplement, not replace, proper coaching training. Like any profession, coaching requires training.

Dear Reader,

The Certified Professional and Master Coaches authoring chapters here are a privilege to know and work with in this, the third annual Coaching Perspectives book.

This collaborative writing effort provides insight on coaching skills and approaches, varied applications of coaching services, and excellent tools and techniques.

The expertise of these professionals is clear. The opportunity to have trained each in coaching and continue to connect with them is an honor.

Kindly let us know how we can be helpful.

Sincerely,

Cathy Liska
Guide from the Side®
Center for Coaching Certification

CENTER FOR COACHING CERTIFICATION

www.CenterforCoachingCertification.com

Info@CenterforCoachingCertification.com

800-350-1678

MISSION:

Enhance your coach training experience with quality, professionalism, and support.

VISION:

A high-quality, ethical norm throughout the coaching industry achieved through leadership by example.

*For coaches,
those thinking about becoming a coach,
and those who receive coaching.*

Table of Contents

About Coaching *by Cathy Liska*..1

A Mindful Approach to Coaching *by Rebecca Cooley*............27

Made to SOAR *by Penny Ducharme*...............................48

Simple Approaches for Positive Change *by Ava Webb*..........67

Sit Quiet and Listen *by Donna Leake*................................86

Coaching with Spiritual Intelligence *by Wendy Glantz*...........104

It All Adds Up – ADD / ADHD Coaching for Teens
by Gina Wilson..126

Your Career Narrative is a Story that Works
by Brian Beatty.. 150

Getting a Grip on Time *by Charlie Kiss*............................. 169

Conscious Leadership *by Jennifer Connell*......................... 189

Coaching in a VUCA Environment *by Maria Van Parys*.........212

Finding Your Ideal Client *by Nozomi Morgan*.....................232

Coaching to Increase Sales *by Jina Fernandez*....................252

ABOUT COACHING
by Cathy Liska

Coaching continues to grow as a profession and is gaining ever more popularity because it works. This chapter is an overview of coaching, how it works, different types of coaches, different approaches, and coaching relationships. The examples are to provide awareness and insight based on coaching competencies.

WHAT IS COACHING?

The definition from the International Coach Federation is, "Partnering with clients in a thought-provoking and creative process that inspires them to maximize their personal and professional potential."

The International Coach Federation is a nonprofit membership organization that serves coaches and their clients alike by supporting self-regulation of coaching with a code of ethics and training standards.

WHAT ISN'T COACHING?

- Coaching is not mentoring. A mentor is a voice of wisdom and experience passing on what they know and giving advice. In comparison, a coach provides process expertise and thereby elicits the answer from the client.
- Coaching is not consulting. A consultant is an expert

that is brought in to analyze, develop a plan, and advise. In comparison, a coach serves as a sounding board and strategy partner so the client explores possibilities and creates their plan of action.
- Coaching is not a mental health service. A mental health professional works to restore an individual to wellness. In comparison, a coach works with an individual who is well and whole to consider what they want and move toward their goals.

WHAT IS THE ROLE OF A COACH?

- *A coach is a strategy partner.* Exploring strategy is essential for creating the best possibility of a successful outcome. The coach challenges and expands thinking so the client fully considers possibilities and develops their approach.
- *A coach is a sounding board.* The coach provides the space for a client to brainstorm and talk through different ideas for effective decision-making.
- *A coach is a provider of perspective.* While it is easy to give advice and suggestions, it is most effective when an individual figures out their own answer. A coach asks questions and uses different techniques for empowering the client to find and consider different perspectives. When a client is truly stuck, a coach will provide several different examples or perspectives to empower their

thinking and planning.

- *A coach is an intention partner.* A coach supports a client by ensuring they are intentional about their strategy and action steps. A coach partners with the client to stay focused and on track.
- *A coach is a motivation partner.* A coach asks a client questions to create awareness of what they do want and their internal motivation, then regularly asks them about the benefit and value of continuing to move toward their goals.
- *A coach is an accountability partner.* A coach checks in with a client on their progress. A coach explores with a client what is holding them back and how they will move forward. A coach also recognizes success along the way and partners with a client to acknowledge for them self what they achieve.

> *"A coach supports a client by ensuring they are intentional about their strategy and action steps."*

WHAT TYPES OF COACHING ARE THERE?

Coaching has application in every facet of the working world, families, and the communities to which people belong. Companies are now developing a coaching culture, and the leaders are using a coaching style of management to enhance results. On a personal level, learning the people and communication skills that are considered basic competencies for a coach helps with relationships at home, in the community, and when serving as a volunteer.

There is thousands of coaching niche areas. Generally speaking, coaching is identified with one of four large categories.

- Career coaching serves individuals looking for a job, or redefining or advancing their career.
- `Life coaching supports exploration and action in areas meaningful to the individual including relationships, family, legacy, life purpose, spirituality, life management, and transitions.
- Business coaches often work with individual owners or managers of small to mid-sized businesses in areas including business management, growth, and sustainability.
- Executive coaches provide services to individuals in the corporate world for skill development, enhanced productivity, transition, engagement, and leadership.

These categories serve as a general way of describing coaching. Each type of coaching may and often does overlap with the other areas. For example, when providing business coaching, personal factors are discussed because the client's business performance is impacted. Executive coaching often includes career coaching because the client is developing their career path in the corporation.

INTERNAL AND EXTERNAL COACHES

An internal coach is an employee of an organization that provides coaching services to other employees. An external coach is hired from outside the organization as a business service provider, whether an individual in business as a coach or a company in the business of providing coaching.

Note: The American Management Association published a study that indicates internal coaching programs within companies are most effective when the internal coaches have external training, when the internal coaching is offered to all employees where the internal coaches work with entry level employees up through middle management, and the executive leadership has external coaches.

> *"...internal coaching programs within companies are most effective when the internal coaches have external training, when the internal coaching is offered to all employees where the internal coaches work with entry level employees up through middle management, and the executive leadership has external coaches."*

FINDING A COACH

As an individual looking for a coach, the process often starts with asking for a referral, searching on LinkedIn, through networking, or by using an online directory of coaches.

When a company wants internal coaches, they identify employees to train in coaching – most often from the Human Resources or Training and Development departments. When a company is hiring an external coach, they often source them through referrals, find them through published books on Amazon, use LinkedIn, or research organizations that are in the business of providing coaching services.

COACHING AGREEMENTS

In the International Coach Federation Core Competencies Number 2 in Section A requires establishing the coaching agreement. The coaching agreement describes the parameters of the coaching relationship.

In the International Coach Federation Code of Ethics Number 15 in Section 3 requires that a coach have a clear agreement or contract with their clients and sponsors.

A coaching agreement provides a common understanding between the coach and the client as to their respective roles, the nature of coaching, logistics of the relationship, and confidentiality.

LENGTH OF COACHING RELATIONSHIPS

The average length of a coaching relationship is one year. Of course there are coaching relationships that are for just a few months and others that last years. Often there is a period of regular coaching followed by periodic coaching. A best practice is to determine a minimum time commitment to the relationship and process, and then continuing while there is benefit to the client.

COACHING PROCESS

There are a multitude of coaching models and processes. Each has value and benefits. It is essential that the coach understand the client and that they adjust to what works best for the client individually.

> *"The number one indicator of success for a coaching relationship is the rapport between the coach and client."*

The number one indicator of success for a coaching relationship is the rapport between the coach and client. It is essential that the process create the opportunity for the coach to get to know their client and for the client to realize they are heard and understood.

A question comes up as to whether coaching covers areas other than the specific purpose for which the coach is engaged. For example, some believe that in coaching sessions, only the job should be discussed. In many cases, this is because the employer is paying for the coaching. In this scenario, some believe that company funds should only be spent on workplace topics. When an individual hires a coach to find a job, the belief might be the coach is there for that one thing, helping them find a job. A different perspective is that when the coaching sessions are limited to only one area, the outcome is also limited. Harvard Business Review found that when an executive coach is engaged, personal issues are also addressed 76% of the time.

A balance between these two approaches is to start with an opening session exploring what the individual wants in all areas of their life. Next, in the second session, work on how that person will create the thinking and habits they want to support their progress and success. Then from the third session on, the focus is about the job or the primary reason for the coaching with the understanding that the client chooses what they want to accomplish in each session and topics other than the primary objective may be included. This approach supports awareness for both the individual and their coach of who the client is and what is important to them. Through this process the client and their coach have a shared understanding of the big picture and develop strong rapport. Then, when other areas in the client's life are affecting them on the job or in other primary interests, the client and the coach are prepared to effectively discuss and strategize. The client is a whole person and what they want in each area of their life influences them in each of the other areas.

> *"The client is a whole person and what they want in each area of their life influences them in each of the other areas."*

How Coaching the Whole Person Applies to All Types of Coaching

Following are several examples highlighting the difference between coaching with a focus on a specific area as compared to coaching the whole person for different types of coaching.

Meet Bill. Bill was an executive in the c-suite (Chief Executive). He was known for being driven and pushing hard for results. Bill had been instrumental in growing the company and the bottom line. Then, to the surprise of his colleagues, Bill's focus, efforts, and results declined substantially. Knowing Bill was all about the job, the other executives gave him pep talks. When the trend continued, the company arranged a formal mentoring relationship. Bill leveled out and at the same time continued to struggle. The Board of Directors started pressuring the executive team as a whole and Bill specifically.

The company hired an executive coach for Bill who focused on the job. The coach served as a sounding board for Bill to brainstorm ideas on how to get back on track. They strategized how Bill could increase engagement and productivity on his team. While Bill's performance improved, he did not achieve his previous level of performance.

Bill decided to hire his own coach because he was feeling completely overwhelmed. His new coach used the whole person approach. In their opening session, the coach asked Bill about all areas of his life. In the process, they explored what Bill wanted at home and at work. Bill's wife had recently died after a long illness. His mom had been helping care for the kids. Unfortunately, she was terminally ill and increasingly less capable. She would soon require care herself. The stresses from his personal life were impacting Bill's work performance. The coach worked with Bill to develop a strategy to take care of his family. Bill hired a live-in who could both provide care for his mom and care for his children. With his family taken care of, he was able to again focus completely when in the office. As a result, Bill's performance at work steadily improved and he again achieved his previous levels of productivity.

Not talking about his personal life kept Bill from developing a plan for moving forward. When the coaching included the whole person, Bill's performance at work was substantially enhanced.

Meet Tonya. Tonya was a team lead for twelve years. She had a reputation for being a loyal, hard worker. Tonya was respected by the people on her team and they worked hard for her as a result. Each day Tonya came to work with a smile and words of encouragement for everyone. Then Tonya and her husband divorced. On her own with the kids, Tonya was struggling financially. The stress was exhausting and as much as Tonya worked on smiling and being positive at work, it was apparent to her team that something was going on.

Fortunately, Tonya's company had employees in the Human Resources department that were trained coaches. Tonya asked to be coached and was given the choice of two different individuals. After meeting with each briefly, Tonya began working with one as her coach. The coach used the whole person approach and started the process with a session where Tonya was asked about what she wanted in all areas of her life. As a result, Tonya shared what happened and then talked about what she wanted now to move forward. With her coach, Tonya developed a budget plan. She created a plan that involved her children in taking care of the house. Tonya felt she again had control of her life. She relaxed and regained her positive attitude.

For Tonya, having a plan for her home life meant that while she was at work, it was easier to focus on the job. Since the coaching addressed the whole person, Tonya's performance on the job returned to her previous high levels.

Meet Elaine. During the down economy, Elaine was laid off from her job. She decided to start her own business. Elaine worked hard and built her client base steadily. As the business owner, she was working 12-14 hours a day. Elaine was successful, and she was stressed. Elaine was overwhelmed. Her family was negatively affected and everyone was on edge. Elaine was afraid of slowing her work pace because she had responsibilities and had to earn a living.

Elaine decided to consider hiring a business coach because she wanted to be more effective managing and growing her business. Elaine also wanted to find a way to be more efficient so she could have more balance between her work and family. When she interviewed prospective coaches, Elaine was thinking that to manage the expense, she wanted to limit the coaching focus to her business management. One coach she interviewed talked about the whole person approach. She explained that in the first coaching session, she plans to ask questions about what Elaine wanted in all areas of her life. The purpose of this was to create awareness of the big picture and all of Elaine's influencing factors. In the second session they work on the thinking and habits that will support Elaine as she achieved what she wanted. Then, in the third session, the focus shifts to the business with a full awareness of outside considerations.

Elaine decided it made sense to be clear on her own priorities, values, and motivations, so she decided to hire that coach. As discussed, with whole person coaching, all areas of Elaine's life were explored and Elaine felt her coach really understood who she was and was on her side as she worked toward her goals. In addition to coaching for managing her business effectively, Elaine worked with her coach on creating balance.

Elaine discovered that having balance in her life meant she made better decisions. She is now relaxed and her business is doing well.

Meet Jordan. Jordan was looking for a job and struggling. A friend suggested hiring a career coach. Jordan did a little research online and then decided that it was just too expensive. Without a job, there simply wasn't any money for extra coaching. With an urgency to be working and earning, Jordan grabbed the first job offered. Unfortunately, the work was miserable and Jordan hated the job. The manager realized

Jordan was disengaged and gave Jordan the choice of quitting or being written up. Jordan quit.

Again looking for work, Jordan decided that a career coach was worth the investment. The career coach then took the time to explore what Jordan wanted and to define values. As a result of this approach, Jordan became aware of what to look for in a job. The career coach became a strategy partner for resume writing and job search strategies. The career coach role-played job interviews with Jordan. Jordan applied for positions that were appealing and with companies that had similar values. Jordan started a new position and was happy and successful.

Meet Kelly. Kelly was ready to retire and became worried about how sometimes people experience declining health and capacity once they retire. A colleague suggested Kelly contact a coach. Kelly was unsure how having a coach applied in this situation and wondered about the return value on making the investment.

At a networking event, Kelly met a coach. The coach offered Kelly a free 30-minute coaching session to experience how coaching worked. Kelly enjoyed the free session and discussed the possibility of coaching for the transition from a full-time career to retirement. The coach explained the whole person process as beginning with a session asking about goals in all different areas for the big picture. Kelly felt talking about goals in all areas was irrelevant because after retirement there was not a whole lot on which to work. The coach asked Kelly how the expressed concern over a decline due to retiring was related to goals in different areas. Kelly thought about it, was still unsure, and then asked to do just a few sessions. The coach declined to take Kelly on as a client because it was not a good fit for Kelly.

After six months of retirement, Kelly called the coach again. Kelly shared a new awareness of how not having goals meant not having direction, which led to doing little or nothing. Kelly asked to start the coaching relationship and to use the whole person approach. As a result, Kelly discovered new hobbies and found personal value in actively pursuing several, and she began active volunteering and traveling, and enjoying retirement.

COMPETENCY OF A COACH

> *Setting the Foundation*
> *Co-Creating the Relationship*
> *Communicating Effectively*
> *Facilitating Learning and Results*

The International Coach Federation publishes 11 core competencies for a coach. These competencies are developed through training, practice, and experience. These 11 competencies are in four areas: Setting the Foundation, Co-Creating the Relationship, Communicating Effectively, and

Facilitating Learning and Results. A case study of a coaching relationship follows with the competencies listed and explained in the context of the coaching.

CASE STUDY ALIGNED WITH THE 11 CORE COMPETENCIES

A retired VP, Edward, was asked to serve on the Board of Directors. With his inside knowledge, he was aware of limitations on the effectiveness of the CEO, David. Edward recommended a 360 evaluation (a performance review completed by supervisors, colleagues, and employees) and follow-up coaching for David. The Board agreed and the HR Director was asked to make the appropriate arrangements. The HR Director hired an organization to provide a consultant that conducted the 360 evaluation and then also served as the coach. Initially, David was resistant to the idea. The consultant / coach scheduled a meeting with David prior to beginning the process.

About the client:
David climbed the ladder in his corporate career of 25 years. He learned that being strong and decisive demonstrated his knowledge, skill, and leadership abilities.

About the coach:
Marie had a successful career in the corporate space and then decided to become an executive coach. She became certified.

Building on her corporate experience and with her connections, she built her reputation as a coach.

THE COACHING AND COACHING COMPETENCIES

    A. Setting the Foundation
        1. Meeting Ethical Guidelines and Professional Standards
        2. Establishing the Coaching Agreement

David asked Marie to explain the coaching process. Marie shared that first she acts as a consultant to administer the 360 evaluation. She explained she was certified in this assessment tool. After administering the 360 evaluation, Marie explained, she planned to switch to a coaching role.

> *"...the role of the coach is to serve as a sounding board, provider of perspective, and strategy partner, and to explore intention, serve as motivation partner, and be an accountability partner."*

Marie explained the role of the coach, discussed the code of ethics, and went through the coaching agreement highlighting confidentiality. Marie explained that the role of the coach is to serve as a sounding board, provider of perspective, and strategy partner, and to explore intention, serve as motivation partner, and be an accountability partner. Marie explained that while the company had the role of sponsor, David had the role of client.

Marie provided David with an agreement that defined the relationship, called for a commitment of three months, and cited the code of ethics. Marie also provided David with a copy of the ICF code of ethics and reviewed several key points. Then they discussed what information to share with the Board of Directors. Marie explained the ethics of confidentiality. The Board of Directors agreed that reporting was not expected, such that Marie was to only share what David wanted shared with the Board of Directors.

Marie explained her coaching process. In the first coaching session, the purpose was to explore the big picture and understand all aspects of what David wanted. In the second session, the focus shifts to how David will develop the thinking and habits to support his success. In the third session, the top priorities are identified, strategy discussed, and action steps planned. David asked questions about the process and decided that it made sense. He stated that while anticipated it to be challenging exploring non-work areas too, he felt comfortable with Marie and recognized the value of the process.

Demonstrating the first two core competencies, Marie ensured David was aware of and comfortable with her commitment to the code of ethics. The two discussed the process and explored the fit for this coaching engagement. The roles were defined and Marie provided a written agreement. The foundation of the relationship was set effectively.

B. Co-creating the Relationship:
   1. Establishing Trust and Intimacy with the Client
   2. Coaching Presence

Marie explained that while the 360 evaluation was being conducted, the coaching starts with David's big picture and exploring what he wants in all areas of his life. Since their initial meeting laid a solid foundation around confidentiality and process, David was comfortable and ready for the coaching session. Marie asked David about what he wanted with a focus on the future. David shared progressively more and found himself talking about things he wanted that he had forgotten long ago. As he opened up, Marie's accepting and affirming responses supported David to relax and trust. Marie probed, used humor, and was completely focused on David. In their second session, Marie explored with David his process for choosing what he thinks about and developing habits that supported his goals. Marie shared her notes on David's goals with him and he realized how deeply she had listened. He said he felt empowered by the way all of his goals were pulled together in one big picture.

In keeping with the third and fourth core competencies, during the first two coaching sessions, Marie built on the foundation established in their initial meeting to develop trust, supported David openly sharing which expanded their intimacy, adjusted with him in the moment, and demonstrated to David that she heard and understood him. Through this process, the rapport and relationship were co-created.

    C. Communicating Effectively
        1. Active Listening
        2. Powerful Questioning
        3. Direct Communication

Beginning with their initial meeting and continuing throughout the relationship, Marie listened with intention. She rephrased and reflected what David said to demonstrate she heard and understood. This also helped David because when he heard his thoughts summarized, it helped him clarify his own thinking and explore further. Marie asked short, simple questions that were open. She asked probing, clarifying questions and then gave David the space to answer. She modeled open, positive, and proactive exploration. Marie used language that was both respectful and clear. She was aware of David's word choices and blended her approach to fit with his style to further enhance his understanding and engagement. Marie's use of assertive techniques supported David in developing the skill himself.

By communicating effectively, Marie modeled skills that David wanted to develop and she supported the effectiveness of the coaching relationship with positive communication.

"...Marie modeled skills that David wanted to develop..."

D. Facilitating Learning and Results

   1. Creating Awareness
   2. Designing Actions
   3. Planning and Goal Setting
   4. Managing Progress and Accountability

Since David explored his goals in all areas of his life, he was more fully aware of both his considerations and his influencing factors. The session that explored how David will develop the thinking and habits to support his goals laid a solid foundation for his action steps. In ongoing coaching sessions, Marie partnered with David discussing his long-term strategy, goal setting, and planning. Marie checked with David on his progress and served as his accountability partner. The coaching process facilitated learning and results for David.

ABOUT THE COACHING, STRATEGIES, ACTION STEPS, AND OUTCOME

In the opening coaching session, Marie asked David what he wanted. He shared that in his career he wanted to achieve specific growth and productivity numbers on the job, and he wanted to successfully serve as a mentor for two of the VP's that had been identified as potential successors. David also realized he wanted to develop certain skills at work to improve his relationships and enhance outcomes. David shared his goal regarding the amount of bonus he wanted to earn. He listed specific debt he wanted to retire. David was close to his financial goals for retirement and stated exactly what he wanted next.

Then David talked about what he wanted in his relationship with his wife and with his now grown children. David set goals for spending time with relatives and friends. David set specific goals for exercising, weight, and his eating habits. He explored what he wanted in his spiritual life. David listed classes he hoped to attend. He talked about the legacy he wanted to create both at work and with his family. He described his ideal emotional state. David said he wanted to volunteer and named a specific cause that was of interest. He defined what work / life balance meant to him and set goals to create time for hobbies and relaxation.

In the second coaching session, Marie asked David about his barriers to achieving his goals. He thought and then said that his own habits got in the way. Sometimes he was so busy that he forgot to think or do things differently to change what he wanted to change. In exploring how to move past these challenges, David and Marie discussed what it takes to change thinking and habits and how to make that happen. Marie worked with David on his process to consistently choose his focus and to develop the habits he wanted. At the end of the session, David and Marie discussed the focus of their next session – to choose his top priorities and plan his action steps.

In the third session, David asked Marie to review the results of the 360 evaluation, which was now complete. Some of the feedback was painful, and David initially challenged its validity. Marie asked simple, open questions to explore further. David realized that it was more important to focus on what he wanted moving forward. Specifically, David realized that by developing his own emotional intelligence, or EI, he could then improve his relationships. He decided he also wanted to work on his communication skills – listening, language, and the way he asked questions. David became aware that his own goals in fact aligned with the feedback from the 360 evaluation.

During the coaching relationship, David set specific goals for skills he wanted to develop. He explored his strategy and planned his action steps. Over time, David improved his relationships both at work and home. His team at the company saw the changes and appreciated David's efforts. David achieved his growth and productivity goals, and he gave credit to the team for the results.

APPLICATION OF THE INSIGHTS

This chapter is a beginning for understanding coaching and what the process offers. Expand on this with insights around the multitude of tools offered by coaches.

Consultants and mental health professionals offering related services enhance outcomes when a coaching approach is taken or when coaching is offered. Leaders in the workplace benefit with a coaching approach. Individuals expand their possibilities with coaching.

> *"The quality of the coaching starts with the training of the coach, the code of ethics, and their development of the 11 core competencies."*

Ultimately, coaching is a service focused on the client. The quality of the coaching starts with the training of the coach, the code of ethics, and their development of the 11 core competencies. The coaching relationship starts with an understanding of the roles and with the coach understanding who the client is and how they process and decide. Through the coaching process, the coach listens, asks powerful questions, and reflects back what the client is saying. The client is given the space to expand their thinking and develop a strategy. The client chooses their action steps and moves forward toward achieving what they want to achieve.

 Cathy Liska is the founder of Center for Coaching Certification and Center for Coaching Solutions. She values serving as a coach and training coaches. Her coaching niches are Business Development, Communication, and Intentional Living.

As the Guide from the Side®, she is recognized among the best in training, coaching, conflict mediation, and consulting. Cathy has trained, presented, and facilitated thousands of workshops, certifications, and organizational retreats. She freely shares from 25 years of experience in business ownership and management.

To ensure she is current in related areas, Cathy has earned the following: Certified Master Coach Trainer, Certified Consumer Credit Counselor, Real Estate Broker, Certified Apartment Manager, Certified Family and Civil Mediator, Certificate of Excellence in Nonprofit Leadership and Management, Certified in the Drucker Self-Assessment Tool, Grief Support Group Facilitator, Certified Trainer/Facilitator.

Cathy's mission statement is "People". Cathy is known for her sharing insights, experiences, positivity, and information that empowers others to achieve the results they desire.

www.CenterforCoachingCertification.com

A Mindful Approach to Coaching
by Rebecca Cooley

Mindfulness has the potential to radically and profoundly transform lives, namely the lives of our coaching clients. Incorporating mindfulness in coaching is an important and beneficial way to effectively assist clients with moving toward future goals while enjoying and living in the present moment. In this chapter, we explore a mindful approach to coaching, the importance and benefits of this approach, and how to apply mindfulness in the coaching process.

Mindfulness

Very simply, mindfulness is a term used to describe being aware of all aspects of the present moment, including the thoughts, feelings, physical environment, bodily sensations, actions, and reactions that are part of the here and now. Though this may seem easy, we know that the mind is a thinking machine constantly focusing on the past, or anticipating the future. Often, focusing on the present moment, or being mindful, is of secondary importance. We have places to go, people to see, goals to achieve… all of which are worthy of our time, so where does the awareness of the present moment come into play when our focus is usually on the past or future? The challenge is that often there is little awareness of the present moment; if there is awareness, it is brief and fleeting. According to practitioners of mindfulness, life is now. When we stop to think of the profound significance of this statement, we begin to realize that our worry, anticipation, our constant thinking about our past achievements, past pain, or even future successes, are insignificant compared to the present moment. Our goal then is to be aware that our mind constantly drifts to the past and future, and then to bring it back to this moment. Why is this important? Because it is the release of past and future, and focus on the present, that will bring us the ultimate balance and fulfillment that we seek. This is not to say that we cannot have goals and ambitions. Our goals are worthy of our attention; realize that each goal attained was attained through a series of intentional steps, each equally important as the other, and far more important than the overall goal. It is in the individual step that we live our life. It is in the one step that we experience life, we experience the present moment, and we experience what it means to be focused and aware, to be mindful. If we are mindful, we can easily tackle life's challenges and therefore achieve more because instead of being overwhelmed with yesterday and tomorrow we are aware of the present.

> *"It is in the individual step that we live our life."*

GETTING MINDFUL: A PERSONAL JOURNEY

For a large portion of my life, I found myself repeating mistakes and in unhappy situations. I did not know why, and did not know how to stop repeating the patterns, how to stop suffering. In my search for answers, I sought out teachers and techniques to help me understand why I was suffering. Still the answers eluded me. I decided instead to turn my search toward activities that could help me relax. I began taking lessons in Tai Chi, yoga, and meditation. At that time, I knew very little about mindfulness or its benefits. I simply knew that I wanted to feel better. What I quickly learned from the classes was that the seemingly ceaseless mental noise and thoughts that were a huge source of my suffering subsided while I was engaged in these activities. I was more focused and my worries seemed to take a back seat. I didn't understand at that time, as I do now, that what I was experiencing and beginning to cultivate was a sense of mindfulness. I was practicing being in the moment. I continued the practice of yoga for years and even went to weekly meditation classes; I still had not quite grasped the connection or distinction between relaxation and living mindfully. I heard instructors talk calmly about cultivating a sense of peace in our daily activities; I quite frankly thought they had something I could never attain and didn't think was possible unless I was practicing yoga or meditation. The concept of mindfulness eluded me and I often felt that my mind was in control and dictated my mood or my actions.

Then for Christmas one year, I was given *Practicing the Power of Now* by Eckhart Tolle. I read the entire book right away and was astonished at how easily Tolle conveyed how to live in the present moment. I no longer thought of living mindfully as some unattainable goal that was only for really calm people who seemed to have it all figured out. As I began to learn more about mindfulness, the message seemed to be loud and clear: we can experience the peace and joy we seek if we learn to quiet the mind and live in the present moment. The way out of suffering, I learned, is through mindfulness. Through my study of mindfulness and of Acceptance and Commitment Therapy (ACT), I learned that we are not our minds and therefore not our thoughts, emotions, or reactions. I learned that quieting the mind does not mean making it stop producing endless thoughts; it is accepting the thoughts as they arise and allowing the thoughts to pass. I learned that the key to living the life I wanted was to act in ways that were in line with my values regardless of what my mind told me or how I felt. For example, if I didn't feel like exercising or my mind said, "what's the use?" I acknowledged these thoughts and feelings and did as one of my teachers taught me, I took the resistance with me on the treadmill! I learned that the more accepting I was of my thoughts and feelings, the more quickly they began to lose their power. I learned to be very cognizant of my reactions, emotions, thoughts, and behaviors. This level of awareness has led to a profound transformation in my life. I feel more

> *"...we can experience the peace and joy we seek if we learn to quiet the mind and live in the present moment."*

grounded, peaceful, and joyful. I continue to practice yoga and meditation and often listen to the audio version of *Practicing the Power of Now* while I ride my bicycle. I express gratitude as often as I can, and bring myself back to the present moment when I notice my mind is drifting into unhelpful thoughts about the past or worry about the future. I aim to live a life devoted to balance and peace and am intentional about not letting my mind create problems or become an obstacle to achieving my goals. My journey of getting mindful is full of ups and downs, lapses, and ultimately coming back to the present moment. My journey is ongoing. I know now that mindfulness isn't something that only occurs in yoga or meditation classes or only if you are a really calm person. It is something we each have the capacity to attain. It starts with an awareness of the present moment and an intentional focus on the one step we are taking right here and now.

A MINDFUL APPROACH TO COACHING

Through my experience and study of mindfulness, I have come to understand the correlation between mindfulness and achieving one's goals, between mindfulness and coaching. In coaching, the mindful coach helps their client cultivate mindfulness so that they become aware of their reactions, behaviors, actions, emotions, and thought processes. Then they begin to identify how these mental activities affect their lives and ability to achieve their goals. Throughout the coaching process, the coach provides the client with mindfulness and values clarification activities. These activities help the client acknowledge and accept the thoughts and feelings that cannot be changed so that they continue to take actions that are in line with their values and goals. In other words, the coach helps the client become unstuck. This alignment and congruency with their values can help clients feel more satisfaction with their lives and experience a greater sense of joy and peace, along with helping them clear the mental clutter so that they can focus on their goals without their mind getting in the way. Different from therapy or counseling, mindfulness coaching focuses on providing the client tools to help themselves become unstuck so that they can again move forward, live in the present moment, and achieve the life they want.

COMBINING MINDFULNESS AND COACHING: PRINCIPLES AND PRACTICES DRAWN FROM ACCEPTANCE AND COMMITMENT THERAPY (ACT)

Acceptance and Commitment Therapy, known as ACT, is a mindfulness-based, values-oriented behavioral therapy that combines mindfulness and behavioral strategies to help people change and lead lives congruent with their values. Developed in the late 1980s by Steven C. Hayes, Kelly Wilson, and Kirk Strosahl, ACT focuses on teaching people how to identify their thoughts and emotions, accept them, and develop a willingness to take committed action toward goals and values in spite of them. Though ACT is a type of therapy, it is also a coaching model. As coaches, it is common to integrate principles from multiple disciplines to provide the client with a well-rounded coaching experience that addresses overcoming obstacles and taking actions toward goals. It is important to clarify to clients that as a coach you are not practicing therapy and do not consider yourself a therapist, and explain that the principles of ACT that you use have been adapted specifically for coaching.

The core principles of ACT are:
- Cognitive defusion: developing distance from thoughts and emotions
- Acceptance: developing an acceptance of unhelpful thoughts and emotions so that they do not influence you or keep you stuck
- Contact with the present moment: developing a sense of awareness of the here and now
- Observing the self: accessing a deeper sense of self that transcends the mind and body
- Values: helping you identify what is most important
- Committed action: helping you set goals in accordance with your values, and take action toward those goals

Each of the core principles of ACT can be used to provide a more mindful approach to coaching. Many useful ACT-based activities relating to mindfulness, values-clarification, and defusion can be found in Richard Blonna's book *Maximize Your*

Coaching Effectiveness with Acceptance and Commitment Therapy. For example, I assist my clients with distancing from their unhelpful thoughts and emotions (cognitive defusion) by using the Defusion Exercise: The White Board. In this exercise, I prompt the coaching client to write down unhelpful thoughts that their mind is creating on a white board or piece of paper and then I ask them to physically distance themselves from the paper and thoughts. The purpose of the exercise is to demonstrate that the thought is a separate mental formation and does not represent the identity of the client. I have learned that the purpose of using ACT principles in the coaching process is not to help the client eliminate the negative thoughts and emotions, instead it is to help them accept that the mind will inevitably come up with ideas, problems, or unhelpful thoughts. The key is not to stop the noise and instead to accept that it is part of what the mind does. Instead of resisting the thoughts and feelings, the client learns to accept them and continue to take action toward important values and goals. After all, whatever we resist persists. According to ACT, the coach's role is to assist clients in developing greater acceptance for what they cannot control (i.e. their thoughts and emotions). With the realization that they are not the thought, and the acceptance that their mind will unlikely stop producing illogical and unhelpful thoughts and emotions, the coach will help the client realize that they are in control of one thing, their behavior. In order to help

> *"...they are in control of one thing, their behavior."*

the client reach the point where they are acting in ways congruent with their values, the coach will help the client cultivate a connection to the present moment and clarify their values through additional ACT exercises. For example, Blonna provides the Values-Clarification Exercise: Sorting the Mail activity. I have used this exercise to help clients identify their values by prompting them to list their values relating to ten major life categories (i.e. intimate relationships, family relationships, friendships, work, health, etc.) on individual cards and sort the cards into ten large envelopes. I have learned that helping my clients identify what they value allows them to easily decipher helpful from unhelpful behaviors that either lead them toward or away from their values.

REASONS A MINDFUL APPROACH TO COACHING IS IMPORTANT

Our lives unfold in the present moment. A mindful approach to coaching helps the client focus on the journey, the step they are taking right now in this moment, while moving toward their goal. This allows them to experience continuous and regular achievement of their goals and cultivate a sense of empowerment that will help them maintain their commitment. According to Dr. Russ Harris, author of *ACT Made Simple*, a person's feeling of well-being is in direct proportion to how mindful they are and the action they take. I take this to mean, that once the client has clarified their values, each step in the direction of their values will be the most important step because it will be intentional and it will be in line with what they truly want for their life. As coaches, we can help our client's realize that the small step they are taking at this moment is not a waste of time, rather it is a significant and important action. If our client's are able to focus on the many small actions they are taking one moment at a time, they will most likely experience a sense of satisfaction and fulfillment on a regular basis.

BENEFITS OF A MINDFUL APPROACH TO COACHING

Incorporating mindfulness into your coaching practice will help clients increase present moment awareness. When an individual is more aware of the present moment, they are acutely aware of their thoughts, emotions, and behaviors. As they become more aware of their internal experience, and their values, they develop an ability to discern helpful thoughts and behaviors from unhelpful thoughts and behaviors. With this level of discernment, the individual is able to accept the unhelpful thoughts they cannot control and choose alternative behaviors that are in line with their values. The ultimate benefit of mindfulness is that the client is fully present, connected, and focused on their internal and external experience. While practicing mindfulness, the client begins to understand

> *"The ultimate benefit of mindfulness is that the client is fully present, connected, and focused on their internal and external experience."*

the relationship between their thought processes, behaviors, feelings, and goal achievement. They are better able to regularly evaluate whether their thoughts and actions are in line with their values and then take alternate action that leads them toward their values and goals. They are no longer held back or stuck in unhelpful thought and behavior patterns so instead are free to move forward. A sense of balance and peace are experienced because the client is no longer resisting their thoughts or choosing unhelpful behaviors.

Practicing mindfulness as a coach allows us to stay focused on the present moment while in a coaching session with a client. When we are focused, we are attentive to the client and can more easily recognize unhelpful thought patterns. This will help with listening and communication skills as we offer new perspectives and assign coaching exercises to help our clients with their specific goals.

How the Coach can Apply Mindfulness in the Coaching Process

I have combined my background and training in coaching, mindfulness, gratitude, and ACT to develop a mindful approach to coaching. It incorporates principles from multiple disciplines and assists clients with cultivating mindfulness, overcoming obstacles, and reaching their goals. A mindful approach to coaching helps the client focus on living in the present moment while working toward future goals. It includes guided meditation, gratitude, visualization, and various mindfulness techniques. In *Maximize Your Coaching Effectiveness with Acceptance and Commitment Therapy,* Blonna (2010) uses a six-step model as a guide outlining how coaches can apply ACT in their coaching practice. Blonna's steps include discussing the approach to coaching and establishing clear expectations, explaining key concepts, identifying values, commitment to goals, overcoming obstacles, and taking action. In my coaching practice, I have learned that incorporating these steps is helpful because it creates a strong foundation for the coaching partnership. My clients are able to understand my approach and are continually learning about techniques that they can use outside of the coaching session to help them move forward. I've built on this approach and have adapted a number of the ACT steps and principles to fit a mindful approach to coaching. Instead of six steps, a mindful approach to coaching incorporates ten steps (the first six steps listed below are adapted from *Maximize Your Coaching Effectiveness with Acceptance and Commitment Therapy* Blonna, 2010).

> **Explain Approach:** During the first session, explain your approach to coaching and how you will incorporate mindfulness and values-identification into the coaching process. Clearly establish your expectations and explain that homework is an integral part of the coaching process.

Build Skills: Provide the client with reading materials so that they can understand the various components of the disciplines that you use in your coaching practice (i.e. mindfulness and ACT). Throughout the course of the coaching relationship, use tools, activities, and homework assignments to help your client practice mindfulness, and values-driven action.

Identify Values: During the initial sessions, use a variety of values-identification exercises to help the client explore their values and identify which values are the most important. Once the client's values have been identified, help them recognize any conflicting values causing issues for them.

Commit to Goals: Help your client identify their goals. Evaluate goals with your client to help them determine whether their goals line up with their values. If the goals and values do not line up, help the client rewrite them. Have the client break each major goal into smaller, specific, and measurable action steps. Give each action step a timeframe.

> *"Evaluate goals with your client to help them determine whether their goals line up with their values."*

For example, imagine you have a client named Dan who regularly works ten hour days and is struggling because he feels he doesn't spend enough time with his family. He is often late for dinner and misses many of his son's baseball games. On a values questionnaire, Dan ranked family at a ten, one of his most important values, and he ranked work at a seven. Though both family and work are very important values for Dan, it is clear that family is more important. He wants to set a goal to spend more time with his family. Therefore, his goal might be: Starting Monday, spend more time with family by leaving work by 5:00 pm. each night and being actively engaged with the kids during family time from 5:30-7:00 pm.

Overcome Obstacles: Discuss obstacles with your client. If the client brings up thoughts and emotions that are getting in the way, provide guided activities during your sessions that can assist the client with defusing from these unhelpful thoughts or feelings, and develop acceptance. Explain that acceptance does not mean that they agree with the unhelpful thought or emotion, instead they are willing to take action toward their goals in spite of negative thought or emotion. Explain the process of deciphering helpful from unhelpful actions as they relate to their most important values.

For example, imagine you have a client named Michelle who struggles with regularly telling herself that it's no use going to the gym. In a values exercise, she identified that one of her top values is health. Through coaching, Michelle has identified that she often gets in her own way. By helping her defuse from the unhelpful thoughts, Michelle is now able to acknowledge and accept that she has these unhelpful thoughts and may have them for some time, and she doesn't let them stop her anymore. She takes actions in spite of her thoughts and feelings.

Take Action: Help the client realize that they have control of their behavior. Regardless of what their mind is telling them, they can control what actions they take and continue to meet their goals.

Just Breathe: Start each session with a brief guided meditation that focuses on the breath. This allows the client to relax and focus on the session.

Be Present: Use mindfulness exercises both during the session and as homework assignments. Keep in mind that mindfulness exercises are not intended for relaxation. The intention is to help the client practice detaching from their thoughts and emotions and help cultivate an awareness of the present moment. After the mindfulness exercise, debrief with the client and ask them for feedback.

Give Gratitude: Toward the beginning of each session, ask the client what they are grateful for in their lives. The intention is to help them realize what is positive about their present circumstances. This focus on gratitude can be used by the client in daily practice, and can cultivate a sense of fulfillment in their lives.

Visualize Success: Throughout your coaching sessions, use visualization exercises to help your client truly see their goal and most importantly take action toward it. Visualization can take many forms. One involves asking the client to imagine the entire sensory experience of achieving their goal. Though the outcome is to be determined, it is important for the client to have a clear image of their aim or goal. Another visualization technique involves asking the client to either draw pictures or find pictures online that depict what they want for themselves. They will use the pictures to create a collage that they will post in a highly visible area in their home. Reinforce to your client that the purpose of the collage is to provide a regular and continuous visual representation of their goals, which will help them stay focused and committed to taking continuous and regular action steps.

HOW THE CLIENT CAN APPLY MINDFULNESS IN PRACTICE

As part of the coaching process, clients will complete activities between sessions that will help them develop their mindfulness skills. The homework will revolve around present moment awareness, identifying values, and detaching from unhelpful thoughts. Encourage the client to practice mindfulness throughout the day during both routine and challenging situations. As with any skill, the more practice the better.

CASE STUDY: MINDFULNESS COACHING WITH JILL

Jill understands the importance and benefits of mindfulness. You have asked Jill to participate in activities that will cultivate her mindfulness skills and help her live the values-driven life she wants.

In the morning, Jill starts her day with gratitude by thinking of all the things she is grateful for. She then spends five minutes meditating alone in a quiet space in her house. While she is eating her breakfast, Jill participates in an active mindfulness eating exercise focusing on the colors, textures, aroma, and taste of the food.

As she drives to work, Jill takes notice of her shoulders tensing as she merges with traffic on the highway. She acknowledges and accepts her feeling of tension and does not try to resist it or stop it. She continues to focus all of her attention on the task at hand, driving.

At work, Jill is presented with a challenging situation with a co-worker who is upset with Jill for missing a deadline. Although the co-worker is mistaken, Jill is shaken by the accusation. Instead of impulsively acting on her urge to settle the issue by going over her co-worker's head, Jill remembers that one of her top values is work. Rather than undermining her co-worker and creating an unpleasant work environment, Jill decides to speak to her co-worker directly to resolve the issue. She also decides to wait an hour because she knows that some time and distance from the upsetting situation to cool down helps so that she can communicate more effectively. Before she meets with her co-worker, Jill acknowledges that her mind has produced an endless stream of scenarios of how the conversation will go. She observes the thoughts and acknowledges her feelings, and focuses on resolving the issue with her co-worker.

After work, Jill goes home to relax and realizes she is still bothered by the encounter at work. Although it was resolved, her mind continues to tell her she said the wrong thing. Uneasy and unable to rest, Jill decides to spend some time meditating. She puts on some relaxing music and closes her eyes. She allows her mind to produce its thoughts and she imagines them passing by like leaves floating down a stream. She just watches her thoughts as they pass by. She realizes that the uneasy feeling is subsiding because she has given the thoughts and feelings some attention, did not resist them, and was able to put some distance between herself and the thoughts.

A mindful approach to coaching is an important and beneficial way to effectively assist clients with living the life they want, and moving toward future goals while living in the present. Mindfulness helps clients become aware of the present moment, acknowledge and detach from their unhelpful thoughts and emotions, and take valued action toward their goals. When an individual learns to be mindful of their internal experience and take note of their thoughts, emotions, and behaviors, they can ultimately begin to evaluate whether they are helpful or hurtful. While they cannot eliminate their hurtful thoughts and emotions, they can choose behaviors that are helpful. They can choose to act in ways that lead them toward their values and goals. When an individual is mindful, they give their full attention to the action step they are taking right now. They realize the present is the most important moment, even more important than the goal. They realize the present moment is an end in itself. As an individual develops this sense of awareness, they become unstuck and begin to move toward their goals while remaining grounded in the moment. I have experienced first-hand the benefits of incorporating mindfulness in my daily activities and believe this approach to coaching will profoundly transform the lives of our clients and help them lead more fulfilling lives.

Rebecca Cooley is an instinctive and passionate coach dedicated to helping people propel to the next level. She is the Founder /CEO of Evolve Mindful Living™, Catalyst Action Coaching LLC, and Evolve Institute Center for Growth and Empowerment™. Rebecca facilitates personal growth, mindfulness, and enlightened leadership workshops. She has coached individuals from small businesses and Fortune 500 companies in a broad range of industries. She incorporates principles from mindfulness, Acceptance and Commitment Therapy (ACT) adapted for coaching, strategic planning, leadership development, and Neuro-Linguistic Programming (NLP).

Rebecca is a Certified Professional Coach with an MPA in Managerial Leadership and Strategic Planning. She has completed the NCDCR *Leadership Development Program*, the NC Center for the Advancement of Teaching *Connections Teacher Training Program*, the IPER *Train-the-Trainer Institute Program*, and the Toastmaster's International *Competent Communicator Training Program*.

Rebecca lives in North Carolina with her husband Matt, and enjoys cycling, yoga, and painting.

www.CatalystActionCoaching.com

MADE TO SOAR
by Penny Ducharme

Many of us have had the frustrating experience of a vehicle being stuck in the mud or snow. I had one such experience on a winter evening a few years ago as I was driving home late at night. As I turned a corner, my car just kept sliding on the ice and snow into a ditch. I sat there stuck, unable to move. I tried gunning the engine, and the tires just spun in place, spraying snow in every direction. I wanted to get out of that rut I'd created by spinning my tires, and didn't know where to start. Being stuck in the mud or snow illustrates our own personal lives at times. We get stuck, unable to move forward in our lives and don't know how to take the first step toward reaching our goals. The harder we try, the more we end up spinning our wheels and not going anywhere. Then, we give up and become accustomed to the mundane, everyday routine and forget that we were made for more. It's just too much work to try to move forward. The goals on our personal bucket list become dreams that are never realized. We accept the 'as is' life we are in. We become comfortable in the rut forgetting about the potential within. As coaches, we will come across clients who feel stuck and unable to move forward. It is our job as coaches, then, to help each client recognize that they were made for more and that dreams were meant to become reality.

> *"...dreams were meant to become reality."*

There were three things I wanted on that winter night: to make a plan, take action, and get help. Similarly, there are three important components to setting and reaching our goals that will help us and our clients fight the inner battle, get out of the rut, and take to the skies.

THE MIND

I live on a lake and have observed many ducks over the years. Ducks dive head first into the water to find food. Just like ducks that dive into the water to go after what they want, we, too, benefit to first use our head to set our target. So, the first component in learning to soar is the mind: *setting the target.*

Sometimes, the hardest part in getting 'un-stuck' is setting the goal because there are so many things you want to accomplish. Think about what it is you want to accomplish. What is one target you want to hit? What is in your sight? A target is something you can see in the distance. It may seem far off, it is attainable.

If you don't know where to start with setting your target, think about the major life areas: physical, mental, professional, relational, financial, social, and spiritual. When you first look at that list, which area of life jumps out at you that you want to change or improve? Hopefully, this will give you a place to start.

This is a great tool, one that I've used myself and with clients, to get an overall picture of where you want your goals to be and where to begin working. Rate yourself on a scale of 1-10 as to your satisfaction level in each life area. Once you discover an area (or areas) where you feel dissatisfied, you can begin to look closer at how to overcome the 'stuck' feeling for that part of your life wheel. Examining your life areas will give you a greater sense of where to begin setting goals.

In reaching your target, there are three things within your mind that will affect success.

Focus

Often times, the target seems unattainable or too big. It's necessary to break it down into smaller parts and get rid of distractions. Another fact about ducks is that they have very keen vision. That is what you want when you set your goals. Keen vision focused on your target.

> *"Keen vision focused on your target."*

Have you ever noticed what happens when a bread crumb is thrown into a duck pond? Every duck frantically goes after that crumb. Nothing is going to stand in the way of the duck and the crumb if they can help it. That's focus! Think of it like wearing blinders to keep your focus straight ahead, keeping that target in your scope. When you look through a scope, one eye is closed in order for the other eye to truly focus on the target. It narrows your vision and helps you concentrate on the target in front of you.

ATTITUDE

The second thing in your mind that will affect whether you hit your target is your attitude. Are you a glass half empty or half full kind of person? I recently saw a Facebook post that stated, "technically, the glass is always full – half water, half air." This is something I personally struggle with. The end result seems so far away, it's easy to become discouraged.

When I started running several years ago, a friend and fellow teammate of mine shared this piece of advice: 'When running up hill, look only three feet in front of you, and the road will look flat.' Hills are a tough part of running, and I was up for anything to make it easier. When I applied this principal, it worked, and still does today. Eventually, focusing on only a few feet at a time brought me to the top of the hill.

I shared this story with a client, and she said that it was this concept that helped her the most. For her, looking three feet in front of her was focusing on one day at a time rather than getting overwhelmed by the busyness of the entire week.

By looking only three feet in front of us, our attitude will become more positive, and we'll gain confidence and be able to observe progress in reaching our goals. And, before we know it, we'll be at the top of that hill.

CONFIDENCE

The third thing that will affect the success in your mind is your confidence. Belief in yourself and your ability is a huge part of reaching your target. I often tell my children, "You are smarter than you think you are." Don't be afraid to try. You have to believe you are capable of reaching your target, that it is indeed possible.

> *"Belief in yourself and your ability is a huge part of reaching your target."*

There is a sign that hangs on my daughter's wall that says: "You are stronger than you seem, braver than you believe, and smarter than you think you are." I have her say that almost every day as she leaves the house for school. It is true for all of us. We must believe in the strength that is within, and the ability that God gave us to accomplish what we set out to.

Think, again, of those ducks in the pond. Have you ever noticed that when a bread crumb is thrown in a duck pond, every duck frantically goes after it like it's a steak dinner? Even though there may be a dozen ducks in that pond, each individual duck is not hindered. Each individual duck keeps going after that crumb, even if failure happens time and time again.

Recognize Your Strength

I saw a picture on the internet the other day of a donkey tied to a plastic lawn chair. I didn't catch the caption underneath the photo; it reminded me of the strength we have within that we don't tap into. The donkey could easily walk away pulling the chair behind him and instead he stays tied to the chair because he doesn't think he has a way of escape. When we get stuck, we don't recognize the strength within to break free of old habits or to change a mindset and go where we want to go. We hold ourselves back when a way out is right in front of us.

The Feet

The second component in reaching our target is our feet: *stepping forward*. This is where we begin to take small steps forward. In order to reach your target, you want to literally *step* forward, not run. This is where the breakdown of practical steps is helpful in order to reach your goal.

Set Your Plan

In order to begin moving toward your goal, set your plan. You've established your target. Now, how are you going to get there? It's tempting to want to get from point A to point Z immediately, as most of us are not very patient when it comes to what we want. However, in setting and reaching goals, there is a process that will take place over time requiring a series of small stepping stones that will get you to the other side.

S.M.A.R.T. GOALS

I'm sure you've all heard about S.M.A.R.T. goals in recent years. Is your plan specific or significant? Is it measurable? Is your target attainable or achievable based on where you are? Is it relevant or realistic based on your gifts, talents or resources? It is time-based or tractable?

As you take small steps, it's important to analyze each small goal along the way against the S.M.A.R.T. process as a check and balance system.

Think of reaching your target like a funnel. When pouring water into a funnel, a lot goes in the top, and only a little comes out of the bottom until it is empty. You start with an overall goal, then funnel down to the specifics of meeting that goal. For example, if you want to begin an exercise program, put that at the top of your funnel. Keep working that down to the small

"You start with an overall goal, then funnel down to the specifics of meeting that goal."

part of the funnel to your starting point. This is the step-by-step process.

What is the first small step you want to take? In starting an exercise program, your first step may be deciding what type of physical activity will work for you, joining a gym, or researching local personal trainers. The emphasis is on a *small* step. Each small step leads to the next, and the next, and so on. It goes back to the three feet in front of you principle. Lately, I've seen many quotes in magazines and on Facebook and other internet sites that emphasize taking the small step. Having success in the small steps gives you confidence and momentum to keep going forward to tackle the next bigger step. We are a fast-paced society, so the concept of slowing down to take small steps seems inefficient or unproductive. It is in the slowing down and focusing where you will see progress.

One of the most important tasks you want to consider as you begin stepping forward, though, is to define your greatest obstacle. As we begin working toward our goals, we *will* run into obstacles. This is where we can easily get stuck, too. One obstacle stands in the way of movement, and we get stuck or give up. Our progress halts. Fear is probably the number one obstacle standing the way of our dreams. Some of us will never do the thing we fear, and it can paralyze us. When that happens, nothing gets accomplished. Recognizing the fears and other obstacles in your path will help you deal with them and find ways to overcome. This is a whole different book chapter, for now it is important to mention that obstacles will arise, and we want to be prepared to face them.

Also, be sure to celebrate the small successes along the way. If you are a big picture person, you might have difficulty celebrating the small steps because your focus is too much on the end result. We are all pretty good at recognizing when we failed, or when that small step toward our goal was a little off. How good are we at celebrating those small milestones? Do you celebrate that you lost two pounds that week, or do you tell yourself it should have been five? Do you kick yourself when you didn't accomplish all on your daily to-do list, or do you celebrate the three or four things you completed?

> *"By recognizing your success in overcoming the small steps, it will actually encourage you to go further."*

It's all about perspective. The 'should have's' can sabotage our progress. Or, the "yeah, two pounds is great...BUT...it could have been more if I just hadn't had that burger and fries on Tuesday." How about instead of focusing on Tuesday, you celebrate all the other days you were disciplined and followed your diet plan? It's okay to celebrate, to be proud of your progress, to jump up and down when you cross over one of the stepping stones toward your goal. By recognizing your success in overcoming the small steps, it will actually encourage you to go further. If you beat yourself up, it will slow your progress and may even stop it all together. Rejoice that you've come this far rather than tell yourself you still have miles to go. Of course, it's important to keep the end result in sight, and remember to recognize where you've been or how far you've come.

THE HEART

Our third component in soaring toward goals is the heart: *accountability*. It is about relationships. This is the absolute key to success, in my opinion. You will achieve greater success by being accountable to someone else as you work toward hitting your target. A support system: family, friends, co-workers, or a coach will increase your chances of success.

We've all seen how ducks fly in the V formation. One reason they do this is that the V structure allows them to communicate more easily. In the V, the ducks easily see each other and stay together. This means also if one duck separates, they are immediately noticed. Communicating and staying in contact with others through accountability will help you reach your destination too.

If is safer for ducks to be in a group than to be alone. Traveling in a group may make it more difficult for a predator to pick out a single prey, or it might startle the predator, allowing individuals to escape. It's harder to achieve our goals alone;

it's easier to allow the predators of discouragement and fear to creep in and attack.

Studies have shown that ducks and birds learn to fly in flocks over time, gaining speed and agility. Mastering quick movements and keeping up with the group takes practice, and stragglers are most vulnerable to predator attacks. Many scientists believe that this is the strength of the group dynamic; the whole is greater than the sum of its parts. Greater success happens when we are accountable to another. Just like a duck, being accountable to another takes practice, and you will gain speed and movement toward your goals at a much greater pace when someone comes alongside of you.

"Greater success happens when we are accountable to another."

During my coaching training, I learned the following considerations related to completing a goal:

Probability of Completion	
Hear an idea.	10%
Consciously decide to adopt an idea.	25%
Decide when to act on the idea.	40%
Design a plan to act on the idea.	50%
Make a commitment to another person to implement the plan.	65%

Have a specific accountability appointment with another person related to implementing the plan.	95%

This chart shows the importance of accountability in achieving your dreams. Without a coach or someone to hold you accountable, the chances of success are not as high. That's why "the heart" is the key to success.

A part of accountability is with whom you surround yourself. A caution related to your support system is to make sure you are involved in positive relationships. Toxic or negative relationships will hinder your growth and movement toward your goals. For example, if you are trying to quit smoking, it isn't be wise to constantly surround yourself with others who smoke. You are setting yourself up for possible failure.

I have a friend who is a breast cancer survivor. When she was going through treatment, her doctor told her to get rid of toxic people in her life, those who weren't supportive or who were negative because he believed it would hinder her healing process. She told me stories of one friend in particular that would make negative comments about her hair loss, or point out the effects of the chemotherapy that didn't need to be mentioned. My friend had to remove this person from her life in order to stay positive and heal. She instead surrounded herself with other survivors who were turning a negative into a positive.

It's the same in reaching our targets. We all benefit from the support of others to help keep us on track. It's too easy to give up. The best strategy against a predator is to put another individual between you and the predator, just like the ducks do in the V formation. Put someone positive between you and the negative. Remember that in the V formation, ducks are surrounded by others giving support, sharing the load, and offering encouragement.

When I was stuck in the snow on that dark night, I was at a loss as to where to begin. A short while after I was stuck, a man came and helped dig me out of the rut. Without his help, it would have taken me twice the time, and I would have become increasingly frustrated. It feels the same when you are trying to reach goals on your own. You might stay stuck longer than necessary and gradually become so frustrated that you give up.

BLACK BELT SUCCESS CYCLE

A few years ago, my children were involved in a wonderful karate program. There was a sign on the wall of the dojo that encouraged participants to, in essence, know their own intentions, plan, have a partner, be consistent, reflect, and recommit.

I love each piece of this cycle because it's a good summary of setting and reaching goals. It involves each part of what this chapter is about: setting a goal (know what you want and have a plan), moving forward (taking consistent action), and accountability (have a success coach). The best part of this success cycle is the constant movement. Reviewing progress and renewing goals implies constant movement and action. Your goals may morph and change, and you'll continuously have new and different goals. Once one goal is met, you will have another, and so on. Look back to your life wheel to continuously evaluate areas where you want to grow.

> *"Reviewing progress and renewing goals implies constant movement and action."*

A TOOL

Here is a practical tool to help you get started with reaching your goals. This process will become easier as you practice it over and over again with each new, small goal.

Some questions or statements to begin with are:
- In which area of my life do I feel stuck?
- Write one *specific* goal.
- What will be the greatest impact from achieving this goal?
- What is the biggest obstacle as I pursue this goal?

Below is a chart answering the specific questions related to reaching the goal.

Example: (goal is to start an exercise program)

Who? Who am I accountable to?	My best friend, Sally.
What? What is my first step?	Buy new sneakers to start a walking program.
When? When will my first step happen? Day and time?	Saturday afternoon at 1 pm; I *will* come home with new shoes by Saturday evening.
Where? Where will my first step take place?	At the mall. I'll shop various sports stores to find the best deal.
Why? Why is this goal important to me?	I want to be healthier so I have energy to keep up with my family and career.
How? How much (cost, time, etc.)? How often (duration, days of week/month)? How many (days/weeks, minutes)?	Approximately $100 for good sneakers; shopping time, approximately 2-3 hours.

For you to fill in:

Who? Who am I accountable to?	
What? What is my first step?	

When? When will my first step happen? Day and time?	
Where? Where will my first step take place?	
Why? Why is this goal important to me?	
How? How much (cost, time, etc.)? How often (duration, days of week/month)? How many (days/weeks, minutes)?	

This chart may not be something you fill out for every single goal. I personally do not write out these steps for every goal I have. I think through each step and have my own system with paper and post it notes that works for me. What's important is keeping the process in mind for each goal you set. Starting small and thinking through the who, what, when, where, reasons, and how of each goal will help you achieve greater success.

> *"What's important is keeping the process in mind for each goal you set."*

REVIEW

In order to break free and soar, remember the three components to successfully achieving your goals:

Mind: set your target. What is it you want to accomplish? What is your goal?

Feet: take that first *small* step. What is the first small step you want to take in order to get closer to your goal? And, take the next small step after that and so on.

Heart: be accountable. Who will help you on your journey? Do you have a support system—a coach or a trusted friend that will hold your feet to the fire?

You were not meant to be stuck, or to be imprisoned in ruts of your own making. Remember, the greatest battles are won or lost in our inner lives each and every day. This is your time to break free from what is holding you back, to spread your wings and fly. You were made to SOAR!

Penny Ducharme is a Certified Life Coach and owner of Embrace Synergy, LLC, a Life Coaching Company. She coaches women in key areas of life such as family, career, and health & wellness. She has a degree in Education as well as a master's degree in Counseling. Penny received her coaching training through the Certified Coaches Federation and the American Association of Christian Counselors. She has additional coaching certifications in the areas of Personal Health & Wellness, Marriage and Advanced Life Coaching. Her passion is helping women, who are overwhelmed with life, realize their full potential and be the best they can be. Penny has written several articles and has been published on-line and in a local newspaper in her area. She also has a weekly blog at www.embracesynergy.com. She enjoys offering free seminars through her church on topics such as Setting & Meeting goals, Overcoming Obstacles, Making the Most of Your Year, and Fabulous You, focusing on fashion and a positive body image.

Penny lives in Maine with her husband, Kevin, and their three adopted children. In her free time, she enjoys reading, baking, scrapbooking and participating in local triathlons and other races. She has a heart for other cultures, as well, and has been to Guatemala several times serving on mission teams.

www.EmbraceSynergy.com

SIMPLE APPROACHES FOR POSITIVE CHANGE
by Ava Webb

As a professional coach, I believe there are many approaches to help a client realize their full potential as the coaching process develops. Coaching clients in a positive, caring, and motivating way is essential. Listening and truly hearing what a person has to say is a significant role of a coach. I strongly believe that each client has a right to truly be heard and the value in that is deeply understood by the client. Coaching generally starts with encouraging each client to explore the areas in which they want to be content, joyful, and successful.

> *"As a person uses or hears certain words each day, he or she starts to believe them over a period of time."*

Utilizing thoughtful and encouraging words throughout the coaching process is highly beneficial to both the coach and client. The more positive words the client hears in a day, the better. As a coach, assisting clients to communicate in a confident, assertive way will be beneficial in helping them understand and develop the appropriate skills to move forward in any area of their life. Positive feedback and providing affirmations are very important. As a person uses or hears certain words each day, he or she starts to believe them over a period of time. This is why an abundance of thoughtful, confident, and valuable words are essential throughout the process of coaching.

Establishing trust and exploring possibilities with a client is inspiring. Coaching calls for ensuring the client is comfortable disclosing personal information. Facing life events will affect people in different ways. Each person has the power within themselves to make choices during life events that can be positive, beneficial, and rewarding. People want to feel safe, calm, and relaxed in order to focus on what their interests are and how they want to proceed. It is appropriate to support the client staying on task.

> *"Each person has the power within themselves to make choices during life events that can be positive, beneficial, and rewarding."*

As a coach, it is our responsibility to recognize what is going on with the client in the present moment. Asking a lot of questions is the best way to do this. As more information becomes available, more possibilities and solutions will be explored with the client. The question that a client has to figure out for themselves is "What do I want?" As the client makes decisions the coach then talks about commitment to reaching the goals set by the client.

Challenging a client in a good way to set goals with time frames, begin to take action, and move forward is a wonderful process in which to be a part. Another question is, "How do I make it happen?" Action is taking place at this point which leads to valued outcomes. The client considers possible strategies, best options, and continues to make solid, measurable plans. As choices are made to improve in any area of life, an optimistic, fresh, new view of oneself and others will start to take place and change will happen.

Each and every person has the ability to explore, realize, learn, and develop new ways to set goals, take actions, and move forward. The momentum to achieve goals is forward.

Through the coaching process a client develops a positive outlook and new goals are set. The value of achieving the goals builds confidence and momentum. Managing and achieving realistic goals will become more natural.

My job as a coach is to explore with the client the objectives that they want to achieve so they set realistic short and long term goals, and to encourage and motivate the client to keep moving forward while managing what is going on around them at the moment. There are different areas to explore with clients so that they can choose and move toward what they want. My intention as a coach is to assist the client in exploring multiple options and solutions so that they can effectively achieve their stated goals. When the client expresses interest in achieving specific goals and wants to strengthen their skills, as a coach I encourage the client to talk and explore each of the goals as they arise, ultimately defining what they want and how they will achieve it. My mission is to support and empower each client from within and maintain the client's forward momentum.

SELF-AWARENESS

Self-awareness is a significant factor in developing goals and action steps because insight into one's self creates awareness of priorities. Self-awareness means having the ability for self-reflection and the ability for independence. Exploring and becoming more aware about one's self is the start of the process of moving closer to knowing exactly what you want and how you want to do it. This includes discovering new information, renewing mind-sets, and learning strengths. Self-awareness also empowers the client to think about beliefs, morals, and values along with thoughts, feelings, and responses in their daily lives. Because of this process, a client will begin to understand themselves and others more clearly. At times expanding awareness of how they may be perceived by others benefits a client for developing their strategies. Alternate approaches towards others and interactions in the present moment can be explored as different situations arise.

> *"Self-awareness also empowers the client to think about beliefs, morals, and values along with thoughts, feelings, and responses in their daily lives."*

With self-awareness, a person can intentionally focus on the present moment and attention is on immediate thoughts, current emotions, and how best to respond. Important information will be heard and achievements will occur. The more a person learns about who they really are, the easier the process becomes to make positive decisions that are beneficial to them in the present moment. The more a person honestly answers the following questions, taking plenty of time to think about each one, the better the chance of achieving their goals: What is my intention for each decision I make? and How will my decisions affect me in a positive way?

PHYSICAL HEALTH

Physical health and proper nutrition are such important parts of our daily lives. As a coach, having an open conversation with each client about personal lifestyle choices is important to explore. As each client focuses on positive choices such as daily exercise, proper nutrition, the right amount of rest and sleep, the client realizes the wonderful benefits. Each day the intentional decisions to eat healthier, keep the body moving, and get plenty of rest and sleep are very rewarding. There are many ways for every person to be physically active such as walking, biking, swimming, jogging, sports, dancing, and any other activity that keeps the body moving. The key is to make it fun!

Nourishing our bodies with healthy foods that are colorful, tasty, and fun to eat is easy to accomplish each day. Take the time to smell fresh fruits, feel the various textures of vegetables, and intentionally enjoy cooking and eating each meal or snack each day.

EMOTIONAL HEALTH

Through exploration with the coach, the client discovers various ways to maintain emotional health. Each client considers which activities, relationships, and events will positively influence them and how they want to apply self-discipline in their choices. Learning and developing new ways to actively participate each day in personal emotional health is very important and leads the client to engage in meaningful and creative solutions.

> *"Learning and developing new ways to actively participate each day in personal emotional health is very important and leads the client to engage in meaningful and creative solutions."*

CONFIDENCE

Confidence affects behavior, posture, body language, the way we speak, and other areas as well. Self-confidence is a value that each client can learn. As positive accomplishments occur, strengths increase, and confidence goes up. The client prioritizes what areas are most important for them to develop through the process of coaching and the coach encourages their awareness of successes.

Resilience

Resilience is a quality that each client can discover through strength and encouragement. The choice to keep moving forward in spite of what is going on in the moment builds resilience. As life events happen, the ability to maintain composure, resolve concerns, and keep an optimistic outlook is effective. Resilience is a positive way to maintain a forward focus on new goals.

Developing Strengths

> *"Exploring strengths along with, talents, skills, and knowledge will increase self-confidence."*

Developing strengths is important for each client to plan during the coaching process. By realizing and understanding what strengths a client has, the coach is able to empower that person to utilize them in appropriate situations each day. Exploring strengths along with, talents, skills, and knowledge will increase self-confidence. It is very significant when a client spends time with other people who inspire and positively motivate them. How does a person know all that they are capable of accomplishing? The answer is already within: free will and being courageous and strong enough to take the first step.

OPTIMISM

Optimism is positive thinking. Experiencing life with a cheerful and confident outlook is so rewarding. Because optimism can positively affect thoughts and health, this is a good quality to have and to explore during the coaching process. By maintaining an optimistic viewpoint each day, realistic goals can be achieved. Another good quality that optimism leads to is increased resilience. Internal moods can be disassociated from external circumstances, which leads to building up resilience. When faced with life events many thoughts, emotions, and responses take place. With a positive outlook, making decisions that are clear and intentional becomes easier and natural. The daily decisions that an individual makes allows that person to take full responsibility for their actions, behaviors, and responses. Making constructive choices that are helpful in fulfilling daily goals is beneficial. Learning new and efficient ways to make decisions will become easier. Each step towards accomplishing the daily goals, no matter how small or big, will begin the process of confidence and achievement. Because the small goals are complete, then striving for bigger goals will naturally seem easier. This is a huge step towards achieving a sense of confidence, a can do attitude, and creating more meaning in a person's life.

Relaxation

Relaxation is a very important necessity of life so that the mind, body, and soul can feel rejuvenated, refreshed, and energized. There are many different ways to relax and to develop the ability for relaxation as a skill. Each person makes the choice of what relaxation means to them; what to do and how to do this is unique to each individual. Some people utilize relaxation techniques such as yoga or meditation while other individuals play sports, enjoy outdoor activities, read in a quiet area, get a massage, or listen to music. A long, hot bath or shower is very relaxing as well. There are many wonderful choices for a person to feel relaxed. Setting aside a certain time each day is important to do, even if it is for only thirty minutes. Individual creativity and exploration in this area will be very beneficial and, after all, who knows a person better than themselves?

Healthy Boundaries

Healthy boundaries between friends, family, classmates, colleagues, and even strangers are important for each person because healthy boundaries support healthy relationships. Healthy relationships provide a support system and positive focus. Boundaries can be set in person, on the phone, or in many other ways so the client feels comfortable. For example, setting times to visit on certain days or meet any other way that works is up to each person to decide.

One aspect of healthy boundaries is how people communicate with each other. It is important to know it is ok to interrupt or disengage when communication is disrespectful.

A physical personal boundary is like an invisible bubble that surrounds a person and is their personal space. In the United States, this means about an arms' length all the way around the person. Usually when someone else besides close family and friends approaches our personal space or is within this invisible bubble without approval, this is considered an intrusion on one's personal space.

Setting clear boundaries in a loving, caring way will be worth the time and effort. Healthy boundaries improve confidence in oneself as well as helping to develop a more defined self-concept. With healthy boundaries, communication becomes easier and relationships are more fulfilling. A client has more stability and control over everyday situations, which is valuable.

The following information is important to think about while setting personal boundaries: Each person has the right to personal boundaries. Taking care of one's self and feelings' before others is important. Saying no to others is fine. Telling others that emotional or physical space is expected is acceptable. Have trust and belief in oneself and others.

> *"Each person has the right to personal boundaries."*

COMMUNICATION

Communication in any type of relationship is an evolving process. Communication within any relationships is very important and, in my opinion, the most important influence on how the relationship will carry on. By using certain words that are constructive and meaningful, the conversation will be more productive and enjoyable. Use positive words each day to develop a new and meaningful way of communication. As a person intentionally uses certain words that are constructive and inspiring, others will listen with more respect. Examples of positive words to use are: Appreciate, Beneficial, Confident, Determined, Excellent, Fantastic, Genuine, Happy, Intelligent, Joyous, Kind, Loving, Motivated, Natural, Optimistic, Positive, Qualified, Respected, Self-reliant, Thankful, Unique, Valuable, Wonderful, Youthful, and Zest.

ORGANIZATION

Organization will assist a person to feel orderly and efficient in their environment as well as being prepared for daily events. When the space surrounding a person is well-organized, a sense of order is in place. Knowing where something is saves time. Organization will be a contributing factor in preparing for daily, weekly, and monthly activities, plans, goals, and appointments. How and what each person decides to organize in their environment and daily lives is a step toward making a difference.

TIME MANAGEMENT

Time Management is effective for many reasons. Utilizing time in an efficient and effective way is rewarding. Our time is precious so managing the when and where is valuable. When a person learns to use time wisely, events and activities are more enjoyable in the moment. Happiness also increases. Putting time aside each day for just a few minutes to think pleasant thoughts will help reenergize your mind and body and a sense of calmness will take place.

CHOICE

The Power of Choice is amazing! The choices made daily by each person will have some form of impact on someone else. The more positive choices that are made, the more positive energy will come back. So many choices are made each day by every single person in the world. Think about how much power we have as individuals to make a difference in our own life and in the lives of others by making positive choices.

> *"The more positive choices that are made, the more positive energy will come back."*

BALANCE

Balance in all areas of life is essential. Having a solid balance means spending quality time doing what is most beneficial and important to each person. Balance has different meanings to each individual. Prioritizing is significant in deciding what that balance is for each individual. Some of the areas to be mindful about in creating a balance in life are: mind, body, spirit, social, financial, activities, and profession. Each one of these areas can be thought about in detail to determine in what order each are placed as a priority. Once priorities are established, the process begins in deciding how to establish a balance in each area.

MOVING FORWARD

Choosing to move forward is the key in living life in the present moment. Intentionally being fully present and living your life in the here and now can improve so many areas in everyday situations. By having an open mind to new ideas and possibilities, you are paving new paths to meet your goals and this is very exciting. Thoughts, ideas, and responses to everyday life will have a fresh outlook.

Each person has a choice to live their lives in a fulfilling, joyful way. Taking a step to do so takes commitment, confidence, and belief. Sometimes moving forward calls for changing habits. To change a habit takes time and persistence. Because of the new paths the client will be exploring, exciting and beneficial challenges are ahead.

The joy of coaching is being fully present with the client during each session. The moment that the client is sharing their thoughts and decides they are going to make a commitment to move forward and achieve their goals is so rewarding. Knowing that in some way I supported the efforts of the client to discover what they want and how to get there is very gratifying. Thinking clearly about what one wants, the time frame to achieve them, and how to make them happen are steps towards success whether for a small or big goal. Each person will define success in their own personal terms and the achievements will feel wonderful.

Live each day with a purpose! Each moment is truly a blessing and sharing laughter, kindness, and patience with one another will make each day amazing.

> *"...each of us has the ability to make choices that are positive and rewarding."*

Each and every person will make thousands of choices throughout their lifetimes. Each choice we make can lead us closer to our goals in life. Every positive decision we choose can also take us forward on a path so that we are content, confident, and happy. Facing life events that we do not fully understand with courage is a choice. The good part is that each of us has the ability to make choices that are positive and rewarding. Results happen, goals are reached, and moving forward is an action towards success. One positive step forward leads to more encouraging choices along the way.

The world keeps on moving whatever is going on around us in life. Make the choice to enjoy each and every day and be very thankful for the things we can control. A wonderful realization is that the only person that can make the choice to set goals, take action, and move forward is one's self. This is a great and freeing thought to have because of the power it creates within. Each of us has the same amount of time, twenty-four hours each day, to make the best decisions in life to reach our goals. Keep the momentum moving forward, the confidence up, and self-worth very high. Intentionally making positive decisions each and every day will make a huge difference in how each person interacts and responds to one another. We all deserve the best out of each day we are given as a gift.

> *"Intentionally making positive decisions*
> *each and every day*
> *will make a huge difference in*
> *how each person interacts and*
> *responds to one another."*

QUESTIONS TO EXPLORE

What do I want to accomplish at the present moment? Write down ten goals that are priority at this present moment.

How am I going to accomplish my goals? Brainstorm and write down five ways to accomplish each goal.

What inspires me the most? Write down names, quotes, places, books, and anything else that inspires you and the reasons.

What is my motivation? Write down what motivates you to fulfill your goals.

What do I want to accomplish in one year? Write down five goals that are priority along with several ways to accomplish each.

What do I want to accomplish in three years? Write down five goals that are priority along with several ways to accomplish each.

What do I want to accomplish in five years? Write down five goals that are priority along with several ways to accomplish each.

Affirmations to Use

Self-confidence: I am confident. Each day I am naturally aware of my emotions along with physical sensations in my body. Because I am focused on positive thoughts each day I am mindful of my intentions when I make a decision.

Courage: I have courage. I am responsible for my thoughts, feelings, and behaviors. Because I am centered and strong I am free to make decisions for myself.

Kindness: I am a loving person who is naturally present for others and easily relied on because I have a positive perspective of others around me.

Interactions: Because I am conscious of my intentions as I interact with others, I am personal, specific, and naturally take action from the healthiest parts of my personality.

Positivity: I choose to be positive and proactive.

Ava Webb is a Certified Professional Coach with a Bachelor's in Interdisciplinary Studies with a focus on Psychology, Health, and Education, and a Master's in Mental Health Counseling from Webster University. Ava has over twenty years of experience in marriage, family, and parenting services. Areas of specialty are transitions, life events, confidence, and purpose.

Ava created Forward Effect for professional coaching on the basis of positivity and motivation. Because of her life events and making choices, she knows the value of confidence and resilience. She believes whatever is going on, an intentional choice can be made to maintain an optimistic viewpoint.

Her personal mission is to empower others to realize their potential by setting goals, taking action, and moving forward. Each client is empowered to explore what they want, develop more self-awareness, and decide for themselves what steps to take to reach their goals. Being a part of the process with each client as they move forward is a joy for Ava to experience.

Ava cherishes time with her family and friends spending time at the lake and beach, playing games, cooking good food, and having wonderful conversations. To her they are true blessings.

www.forwardeffect.com

SIT QUIET AND LISTEN
by Donna Leake

In this chapter we will explore how intuition helps create balance in your life and how to use intuition to add value to each session when coaching. First, think of a decision you have made in the past when shortly after you had an uneasy feeling about it in your gut. How about a time when you acted quickly upon something and when you were asked what made you do it your reply was, "Something in my gut told me so?" That was your inner voice, your intuition speaking to you by sending you messages from within your subconscious. Many of us choose to ignore those messages and go with our conscious reasoning. Our past experiences teach us to think about what worked and did not work for us in the past, and then we use those experiences as a guide instead of our intuition. In this chapter, I will talk about the definition of intuition, how to distinguish intuition from your conscious reasoning, my personal experiences, and how intuition led me in the right direction.

WHAT IS INTUITION?

We have heard the term used before; what exactly does it mean? Most of us refer to intuition as our inner knowledge, our inner compass, or our inner voice. Some people even use the term sixth sense. I'm sure you ever heard anyone say that they have a sixth sense about something. What they were telling you was that something other than their subconscious reasoning was giving them information. Whichever word, phrase, or term you want to use to describe it, it all comes down to our intuition.

Intuition is the ability to know something immediately. Intuition is the first thought that comes to your mind when asked a question or making a decision. It is your inner knowledge differentiating what is right and what is wrong for you and leading you to make the best decision for yourself. When faced with decisions, the best thing to do is to listen to your gut. You know what you want, when you want to do something, and how you want to do it. Thoughts and ideas may repeat in your mind over and over again; your intuition will tell you when the right moment is to act upon them. That is why they came up with the phrase "timing is everything". Think of the times when you've rushed into something and had second thoughts afterwards. At times we react quickly for the wrong reasons. Sometimes the pressure to give someone an answer can cause you to have doubts or regrets later on. When we learn to sit quiet and listen, we can actually hear what our intuition is telling us. When our minds are cloudy and filled with noise, our intuition will keep poking at us until we do listen.

> *"It is your inner knowledge differentiating what is right and what is wrong for you and leading you to make the best decision for yourself."*

SIT QUIET AND LISTEN

We live in a busy, fast paced society. Everything is to be done yesterday. We walk around with our heads filled with noise, thinking about all the tasks ahead of us, and worrying about situations from our past. The louder the noise gets, the less intuitive we become. We react on impulse or procrastinate because we don't know what we want anymore. There's too much going on in our heads that it becomes difficult to clearly think and listen. Intuition is our inner compass and it is important to trust where it wants us to go.

When life gets a little crazy it is a good idea to shut down the devices and take time to sit quietly with ourselves. This provides opportunity to become centered again. Take some time sitting by yourself in a park. This is a perfect time for you to be fully by yourself and allow your intuitive feelings to flow. For most of you who are used to running around all day, the first moments your mind will be all over the place, thinking about where you are, who and what is walking around you, things you will want to do when you get home, and what other people in your life are doing at this very moment. As you start to relax, your thoughts will clear, and you will become present with the moment. You are completely with yourself. You can see all the beauty around you, smell fragrances from the flowers, and hear the beautiful sounds of nature that is surrounding you. This is the moment when you are able to have a conversation with yourself again. You can immediately feel how calm and relaxed your body is, as it is reacting and telling you that this is exactly where you are to be at his moment.

As you are sitting or walking through the park, listen to what your body is telling or showing you and become aware of your thoughts as they surface. Emotions from years ago can come to surface. Perhaps you see a woman walking with her elderly mother and thoughts start to stir inside of you. What are you hearing you tell yourself to do? Is it time to reach out to your mother and spend time with her? Perhaps you see two women drinking coffee, talking and laughing with one another, and all of a sudden you have thoughts of speaking to one of your good friends. In this moment, stop and think of all the different ways you can reconnect again and make it happen! What is your intuition telling you to do?

> *"What is your intuition telling you to do?"*

Now do you understand what I mean about sitting quiet and listening to your intuitive thoughts? How many times have you walked or sat in that same park and heard only the conversations that were going through your head, the noise of the person you are with, or from the people walking around you? Allowing yourself to be present with your sixth sense will give you a very different experience.

HOW WILL I KNOW WHEN I AM BEING GUIDED BY MY INTUITION OR BY MY CONSCIOUS REASONING?

When people ask me how will they know when their decision was intuitive or coming from their conscious reasoning, I turn and ask them how much thought went into the decision before it was made and what were they feeling afterwards. Were they feeling good about their decision afterwards or are they now having regrets? Our conscious minds work quickly, so at times it may be difficult to differentiate between the intuitive thoughts and the conscious reasoning. Think of it as this, as soon as we are asked a question, our conscious reasoning pulls files from everything we have learned or experienced in our past and we make our decision based on that knowledge. So, if something worked for us, or someone else in the past, it seems like a great idea to do it again. Our intuition will make the decision for us based on what is good for us in the moment and not whether something did or did not work for us or someone else in the past.

> *"Our intuition will make the decision for us based on what is good for us in the moment"*

As the moment is right for us to go out and do something, our intuition will tell us it is and we will feel excited about it. This is one great way to know if you are making a decision based on your intuition or your conscious reasoning. You will be happy about your decision, days, months or even years later. Are you feeling happy and content with the decisions you have made in your life? These are the feelings that will assure you that you that you went with your intuition.

When we make a wrong decision in life our intuition will keep poking at us, wanting us to revisit thoughts, situations, or decisions we made and make changes that will add value to our lives today and in the future. Have you ever had the same thought come to you again and again every once in a while? Examples: Thoughts of changing your career, wanting to move, or wondering if you are truly happy in your relationship. When we are not where we want to be, our intuition will keep reminding us that there is something we want to change or make happen, while our conscious reasoning will keep suppressing those thoughts that come up every now and again. Our conscious reasoning will find reasons as to why you will stay where you are, and your intuition will have you thinking of ways to make changes and move forward.

Below is an example for you to see how one of my clients allowed herself to be guided by her conscious reasoning instead of what her intuitive messages were telling herself. In one of my coaching sessions, I had her quickly write down what upset her about her husband. After she created the list, I had her right down whatever conscious reasoning she had for tolerating what was upsetting her. Take notice as to how her conscious reasoning was making excuses for everything on her list. One of the things I was coaching her on was her fear of being alone and how it was apparent that her intuition keeps telling her to make changes. In this example, see how her conscious reasoning makes excuses for her so she will stay where she is in her relationship.

Intuition – He doesn't make me laugh.
Conscious Reasoning – It's okay. I make him laugh.

Intuition – He doesn't share the same interests as me.
Conscious Reasoning – It's okay to like different things.

Intuition – He never compliments the way I look.
Conscious Reasoning – I know he loves me anyway.

Intuition – He spends too much time with his friends.
Conscious Reasoning – We don't always have to be together.

Intuition – He never suggests taking me out to dinner.
Conscious Reasoning – It's okay. I enjoy cooking anyway.

> **"Going with your gut means being satisfied with decisions later in life."**

When our Intuition is speaking out to us, it is time to sit quiet and listen. Going with your gut means being satisfied with decisions later in life. This was an eye opener for my client. By switching her way of thinking, making changes, and communicating what she wants to her husband, my client now feels more respected and loved, realizing they can make it work with more communication.

WHAT ARE THE REASONS PEOPLE SUPPRESS THEIR INTUITIVE MESSAGES?

We have all suppressed our intuitive messages throughout our lifetime, and each and every one of us has our own personal reasons. Some of the reasons include being too busy, not in the mood, finances, waiting to do it with someone else, afraid of failure, or afraid of success. Whatever the reason is, it mostly comes down to fear. How many times were you about to do something, then wasted your time contemplating and creating a list in your mind as to all the things that might go wrong? Your intuition knows when you are ready and able to make a move at something. Something inside of you made you think of it, so go with your gut and go for it. As you trust your intuitive feelings, you will see your life change, and you will want to go after more opportunities that world has to offer.

Our past experiences have a lot to do with why we stop and analyze most situations before committing. We have been a witness to so much during our lifetime, and a large percentage was from the people who are closest. Sometimes words that were said to us create roadblocks that prevent us from moving forward. Perhaps the harsh words or a situation shared with a parent, sibling, friend, classmate, teacher, co-worker, boss, or a spouse had us thinking twice about the decisions we make today. The good news is that you have the power to change the negative and replace it with the positive. Below is a list that was created by one of my clients of the negative language that was spoken to her by her grandmother. As you read the lists, take notice to what you are feeling as you read the negative language and what you are feeling as you read the positive and encouraging language. It is amazing how words can affect our thoughts, our decisions, and our lives.

Negative – You can't do it!
Positive and Encouraging – I can do anything I put my mind to.

Negative – You will embarrass yourself.
Positive and Encouraging – All that matters is what I think.

Negative – Did you think this through?
Positive and Encouraging – I know what I want.

Negative – Why would you want to?
Positive and Encouraging – This will bring me joy and add value.

Negative – You will hurt yourself!
Positive and Encouraging – I am capable of taking care of myself.

Can you feel the empowerment that comes from making your own decisions and doing what you want? Replace all the negative thoughts in your mind with positive and encouraging ones, and you will feel confident to move forward. Remember, the negative things that other people say come from their own fears and doubts. They usually think that they are looking out for you and saving you time and energy from failing based on their own past experiences. Remember, that was their experience. Life is all about experiencing and learning new things. So go with your gut, experience life for yourself, and enjoy it!

> *"So go with your gut, experience life for yourself, and enjoy it!"*

WHAT IS THE ADDED VALUE WHEN A PERSON GOES WITH THEIR INTUITION?

When people give themselves permission to be guided by their intuition, they feel confident that they are doing exactly what they are meant to be doing and are heading in the direction they are meant to be heading. They have a clear conscience. Having a clear conscience leaves room to focus on other goals to reach and achieve them. That is the added value.

Below is a true story. I was blown away by this woman's ability to trust in her intuition. I like to share her story with as many as possible so they can see the value added in life when you trust your gut and do what you want in life.

I met an amazing woman one day while I was shopping in her boutique. She told me that it was not too long ago when she used to be a customer here herself. When having a conversation with the previous owner, she was told that they had thoughts of closing it down. Immediately, without hesitation, she asked, "Make me an offer. I want to buy it." Never owning a store before and knowing nothing about retail, she went with her gut and closed the deal. Today, she is the proud owner of her very own boutique. She admits there were some learning curves along the way, and she managed to handle it by herself. There was something inside her, an inner voice that told her to go for it, and she did. With the fun and trendy feel of the boutique, and her bubbly and inviting personality, she is already making it a success.

This is a perfect example of how listening and being accepting to what your intuitive thoughts are telling you can bring you things beyond what you imagine. Things start to happen right in front of your very eyes. To this day, she is happy with her decision she made and has thoughts of starting a second business.

> *"...listening and being accepting to what your intuitive thoughts are telling you can bring you things beyond what you imagine."*

USING INTUITION IN MY PERSONAL LIFE

Learning to listen and go with my intuition was challenging for me as I was growing up. I learned to lean on others for advice and guidance, with fear that I was going to fail on my own. Situations in my past have given me the opportunity to begin the process of trusting myself and making my own decisions. I can remember the times when I sat on my couch for hours just thinking about where I wanted to be in the future, making mental notes of how I was going to do it, and when I wanted to make it all happen. I felt in control and empowered as I saw all my hard work lead to things happening.

I felt good after going with my gut. Most of all, I felt centered. I had a clear head to take on other tasks that added value to my future, such as changing jobs, going back to school, and even starting my own business. These things are possible because I followed, trusted my intuition, and took control of my destiny. For years I felt my intuition poking at me, telling me to go back to school, change careers and do what I loved to do most in life. As soon as I started to look into schools, my fears of working full time and attending college came over me and I stopped searching. My conscious reasoning was saying, "I don't have the energy to spend on college right now." Meanwhile, my intuitive thoughts were saying, "I really want to go back to school and I can make this happen. I know I can and I will." So what did I end up doing? I listened to my gut, found a school, graduated, and changed my career to something that I love doing. I now feel empowered and confident that I can do anything I set my mind to.

The best payback for going with my intuition was marrying my husband. For years I was asked the question, "When are you going to settle down and get married?" My answer was always, "When I feel it in my gut, I will know." In the meantime, life was amazing for me and I was enjoying all that I had and was doing. One Friday night, I was contemplating meeting my girlfriend for happy hour. I had worked late almost every night that week, was exhausted, and had thoughts of cuddling up on my couch that evening to watch a movie. The girls in my office, seeing how tired I looked, were also advising me to stay home and rest. As I was leaving my office and walking to my car, something in my gut was telling me to go and meet my girlfriend. So I went with my gut, gave her notice that I was heading to happy hour to meet up with her, and away I went. About two hours later, there he was, my future husband.

> *"The questions that surface are non-judgmental, open-ended..."*

USING MY INTUITION AS A GUIDE DURING MY COACHING SESSIONS

When I allow my intuition to guide me during each coaching session, powerful questions surface. The questions that surface are non-judgmental, open-ended, and come from me being present with my clients. These powerful questions actually push my clients to think deeper for their answers and move them further along within each session. How do I know when my question is intuitive or from my conscious reasoning? My questions will start to flow without having to think of them while my client is speaking. Think of a time when your friend came to talk to you about a challenge. Were you listening to what they were saying or were you empathizing and giving them advice? When we empathize, we are not fully listening to what the other person is saying. We are immediately thinking of our ideas for handling the situation. Your friend knows what they want, what they are capable of, when they want to do something, and how they are going to do it. When you are intuitively listening you are asking them questions that pertain to them. You are actually removing yourself from their situation.

As a professional coach I am able to detach myself from the situation my client has brought into the session and come up with powerful questions instead of solutions. As my questions begin to flow, so do the answers for my client. My client will begin to think intuitively and is able to discover what is holding them back and tell me how they will make changes.

As I am listening to my client, my intuition is also picking up tones, volume, and the choice of words that my client is using. I notice when someone is being serious, funny, sarcastic, upset, angry, happy, anxious, fearful, disinterested, bored, excited, or thrilled. All of these things are feeding my intuitive thoughts and have an impact on the questions. Being aware when I am hearing their tones, volume, and choice of words, my intuition will direct me to ask a question about what they are feeling at that very moment. I had a client tell me that things were going great with her, and her family was doing just fine. As her voice started to crack and her tone was off, it was obvious that there was a lot more happening. My intuition focused on something deeper and with one powerful question my client opened up and shared, giving her great awareness.

There is a higher level of trust between my client and myself, when they can feel my compassion. Intuition allows me to dig deeper within myself, and feel more than my conscious mind will ever allow me to. Intuition is a powerful tool that brings me awareness to my client's tone of voice, words they are saying, and physical expressions they are using during each session. It added value into my coaching practice, and my confirmations are the wonderful changes in my clients as they move further along through coaching.

Conclusion

My goal for writing this chapter is for people to discover the importance for learning how to trust in their selves again, and to follow their own intuition. Your intuition is there, so listen to what it is saying! Intuition is a gift we all have, so trust and use it. It is there constantly, giving us the information to guide us through life. By going with what your intuition is telling you, you will have peace and balance in your life. You will be able to make better choices just because you will be thinking with a clear mind. Any time you are faced with a decision, please, take time out for yourself to sit quiet and listen to your intuitive thoughts. Put all your fears aside and trust that only you know what is best for yourself. Start depending on you from now on.

I do want to make a clear note before I end this chapter. Although my message is all about the added value when going with your gut, we can also make great decisions with our conscious reasoning. Conscious reasoning can protect us from making mistakes, embarrassment and pain, wasting our money, physically hurting ourselves or other people. Some of my best final decisions were made with my conscious reasoning. My intuitive thoughts kept poking at me throughout the years, telling me to go back to college, and my conscious reasoning created my final decision to follow through. Perhaps intuition and conscious reasoning go hand in hand at times. Do you agree?

Donna Leake is a Certified Professional Coach with a Bachelor's Degree in Psychology. After working years in the field of finance, Donna chose to go back to school for psychology, become certified as a coach, and start a career she loves. Donna now coaches women who want more out of life. Her niches include self-care, relationships, and divorce. Her education in psychology has made it easier to work with the emotions of her clients, and in the end bring out the best in them.

Donna has a love for writing. In college, she was asked by her professor to publicly share her writing at their fall conference. Donna also shares a love for art and photography, which she gets from her father. She took up photography as a minor in college and studied photo history, 3D art and design, and learned how to use a view camera. Her parents created a dark room in their house where she processed her negatives into black and white prints. Donna worked part time at a photo studio where she experienced the business side of dealing with clients.

Donna is married to Bobby Leake and has a son Raymond. Both their love and support have given her the courage and confidence she deserves to make her business a success.

www.donnaleakeclc.com

COACHING WITH SPIRITUAL INTELLIGENCE
by Wendy Newman Glantz

"Spirituality is believing that everyone has the right to draw spiritual energy and to bring that Light into their lives and the lives of others."
Karen Berg, Spiritual Leader
Simple Light: Wisdom from a Woman's Heart

We are drawn to reaching our highest potential. There is something we seek which drives us to achieve and accomplish our successes. Where does information come from which guides us in making multi-million dollar decisions? Is it all based on logic, or is there another driving force, or forces, that guide us? What do we call the driving force, this inner force? Many refer to this internal force as intuition or a gut reaction. Is this based on our logic, or information we have accumulated through our life-experiences? Perhaps it is a stronger force than that, maybe an energy field which we cannot see, feel or touch, rather something we can now call spiritual intelligence.

Reflect for a moment, do you ever ask yourself any of the following questions?

1. What is my purpose in life?
2. How am I accomplishing this purpose?
3. How is my work related to achieving my purpose?

4. How am I seeking a sense of self-fulfillment in my work, in my day?
5. What am I doing that is bringing meaning to my life?
6. What am I doing to help mankind?

Some may have the answers to these questions, and others might not even think about them. Ultimately life leads us toward an awakening, a spiritual revelation which will manifest as one's life's purpose. This happens when you recognize that it is not about the 'me' and it is about the 'we'. You are part of a puzzle, a global recognition, which will ultimately unite and create a world consisting of human dignity and world peace.

WHAT IS SPIRITUAL INTELLIGENCE?

> *"Spiritual Intelligence is one's personal growth in transforming and connecting to one's soul's intelligence."*

Spiritual Intelligence is one's personal growth in transforming and connecting to one's soul's intelligence. It is connecting to the inner voice to help guide you. This spiritual intelligence guides you through your day, week, month, and life. You can even apply spiritual intelligence to your business to find a deeper meaning in your work. By developing spiritual intelligence in your business, or work, you can develop and manifest the soul of your business. This will grow and transform your business to a more meaningful level.

The concept of spiritual intelligence was developed by the thought-leader and author Danah Zohar. She refers to spiritual intelligence as SQ. There are different intelligences that we apply in our daily lives. There is IQ, which is one's cognitive intelligence or intellectual intelligence. There is EQ, which is your emotional intelligence. There is also RQ, which is our relationship intelligence. The concept of SQ is connected to one's desire to connect to a force that is greater than oneself. This force can be considered to some as the light force. It can also be the connection to one's higher consciousness known as God, Allah, Buddha, or whoever you perceive to be your higher power. Spiritual intelligence consists of universal laws that affect how each of us interacts with one another. You can apply these universal laws to help guide you in making better decisions.

Applying spiritual intelligence to your personal and business life gives you the ability to connect to your inner wisdom. Some of the many benefits include beginning to behave in a more proactive manner by treating others with human dignity and respect. In the workplace it creates a foundation of stronger leadership.

Ultimately, you can create inner self-fulfillment which then can transcend and create a global consciousness of worldwide transformation. Additionally, you can apply SQ in your business and create a stronger culture and core values that benefit your business and mankind.

Spiritual intelligence is constantly evolving and has become more clearly defined by Cindy Wigglesworth, the author of *SQ21: The Twenty-One Skills of Spiritual Intelligence*. The SQ21 skill assessment module provides twenty-one skills and tools that help one evolve and connect to his or her own spiritual self. This model has helped create the concept of spiritual intelligence in a more concrete format.

This self-assessment model is divided into four quadrants and applies appropriate skill sets within each quadrant. The four quadrants consist of self-awareness, universal awareness, self-mastery (change), and spiritual presence. The importance of this assessment model is to help an individual with his or her own personal growth. This model has also been applied in business for building an innovative organizational leadership.

How to Apply Spiritual Intelligence in Coaching

There are many pathways for an individual to achieve spiritual growth if he or she chooses to apply spiritual intelligence in his or her coaching practice. It is important when coaching clients that they are made aware of this path so they can achieve their self-fulfillment. Spiritual intelligence is not the practice of dogma or religion. This must be clarified at the onset. It is the transformational process of connecting to one's inner intelligence known as one's soul intelligence. It is exploring and finding the deeper meaning in one's life's purpose. It can be further developed by applying the principles of spiritual intelligence to one's business by developing core values, a mission, and a vision.

By tapping into your soul, you can activate your intuitive ability to help guide you through challenging situations in your life. Some believe your soul has journeyed many lifetimes and contains endless information. By activating or connecting to your soul, you can then connect to a higher consciousness. Allowing your higher consciousness to guide you opens the door to limitless possibilities by activating your creativity.

> *"By activating or connecting to your soul, you can then connect to a higher consciousness."*

THE REASONS, THE WHAT, AND THE HOW

In applying spiritual intelligence to your coaching practice, there are many questions you use to guide your client through this process.

Ask your clients the following questions to begin the process of explaining spiritual intelligence. These questions will begin to open the door for the clients to connect to their inner intelligence, their soul intelligence, and explore a deeper meaning in their lives.

QUESTIONS

The Reasons
1. What are you seeking in life?
2. What are the reasons you are experiencing happiness?
3. What are the feelings you are experiencing?
4. What are the reasons your emotions change throughout the day?
5. What are the reasons your emotions cause you to be reactive?
6. How do these reasons affect your life?
7. How can you change how your emotions affect your reactions?

The What
1. What are your true desires?
2. What are your priorities in life?
3. What do you enjoy about your job?
4. What relationship are you working to create?
5. What is your life's purpose?
6. What will you do to improve the quality of your life?
7. What will you do to help others?
8. What do you value in your life?

9. What are the most important things you have accomplished in your life?
10. What brings you total happiness and joy?
11. What environment do you desire to create and build?
12. What does success mean to you?
13. What is self-fulfillment?

The How
1. How will you achieve your life's purpose?
2. How will you improve the quality of your life?
3. How will you improve the quality of life for others?
4. How will you develop a deeper meaning in your life?
5. How will you achieve success?
6. How will you achieve prosperity?
7. How will you seek self-fulfillment?
8. How will you make a difference in your business?
9. How will you make a difference in this world?

> *"It is important that the client trusts you and feels comfortable to explore these areas of deeper meaning."*

These questions provoke a dialogue which will provide a deeper meaning to your client's life. It will help you build a stronger client-coach relationship. It is important that the client trusts you and feels comfortable to explore these areas of deeper meaning.

WHAT IS PERSONAL GROWTH AND SELF–FULFILLMENT?

In your coaching practice you can apply spiritual intelligence to all aspects of your client's life. A client can realize that life has a deeper meaning beyond just survival mode. You can assist them to abandon their limited belief system and in doing so your client begins to explore a new meaning in life. As a coach, you can help provoke deeper thought from your client about their genuine purpose in life. If the client will let go of all limiting beliefs, fears, and worries, what will he or she want to achieve? Ask, "What is your biggest dream if you had all your personal and financial requirements handled?" What are the possible responses?

Questions to elicit deeper meaning:
1. If you won the hundred million dollar Powerball, and are perfectly healthy, what will you do with all your money?
2. How will the money create love, joy, and/or self-fulfillment in your life?
3. What do you want to be personally self-fulfilled?
4. What does that feel and look like?
5. How will you achieve this self-fulfillment?

In exploring the concept of self-fulfillment the client begins to realize he or she is truly searching for a feeling. A feeling of success, a feeling of accomplishment, a feeling of joy. A feeling of contentment and satisfaction, that aha moment. The continuous feeling of internal harmony and satisfaction. The feeling is acquired by successfully accomplishing a goal or by overcoming a challenge. The feeling is a connection to a higher source. Having a higher purpose allows one to enjoy a feeling of self-fulfillment.

> *"Having a higher purpose allows one to enjoy a feeling of self-fulfillment."*

REASONS FOR APPLYING SPIRITUAL INTELLIGENCE TO YOUR BUSINESS

One can also apply spiritual intelligence to business. This will create an opportunity to bring more prosperity to the company. The client finds a deeper meaning for the purpose of the client's business. The client is exploring and redefining the vision, mission, core values, and culture. The client begins to explore how the business can help others and achieve a higher purpose. Then the client begins to explore and create a new meaning in the business, which ultimately connects to a higher consciousness. By connecting to this higher consciousness the client begins to open new gateways of success and prosperity. Limitations are removed and then the client begins to explore the limitless. The client's consciousness begins to expand, which allows more positive energy to enter and create professional growth and success.

As a coach, begin to probe by asking questions to help guide the client through this process. The client can begin to explore a new meaning in his or her business life. The client can achieve this by applying the process of spiritual intelligence. This is spiritual intelligence in action!

CREATING A NEW PERSPECTIVE

Ask the following questions to assist the client to begin the process in applying spiritual intelligence in business. These questions will help them explore a deeper meaning for their business. They will begin to develop a positive business consciousness.

Questions to Explore the Values and Beliefs You Follow
1. What are your personal values?
2. How do you apply these values in your professional (business) life?
3. How do you apply these values with your co-workers?
4. How do you apply these values in your business relationships with your clients?
5. How can you build on these values?
6. How do you share these values with others?
7. How will you act positively or proactively during your working day?
8. How will you positively motivate others to act that way (your co-workers, colleagues, and business partners?)

9. If you listened to your inner voice, what is it telling you to do right now in your workplace?

Questions on Mission – the Primary Purpose of the Organization
1. What is the mission of your business?
2. How does this mission help others and your clients?
3. How does this mission help improve the world?
4. How can you redefine your company's mission by applying soul intelligence to your business?

Questions on Vision – What the Organization Wants to Achieve in the Future
1. What is the vision of your business?
2. How does this vision help others?
3. How will this vision help improve the world?
4. How can you create prosperity in your company by applying this vision?
5. What gives you the greatest feeling of success in your business?

Questions on Soul Intelligence – the Higher Purpose of the Business
1. Describe the soul intelligence of your business.
2. How can you help develop this intelligence in your business?
3. What are the benefits to your company?
4. What are the benefits to others?

5. How does this help improve the world?

Questions on Core Values that Form the Foundation of the Organization
1. What do you believe are the core values of your business (workplace?)
2. Please list and identify them.
3. How do these core values apply to you?
4. How will you implement these core values in your business?
5. How do these core values help others?

Questions on Culture – the Values and Beliefs Followed in the Business
1. What is the culture you desire to develop in your business (workplace?)
2. How can you redefine your company's culture by applying "SQ" or developing a soul within your company?
3. How will your business grow by doing this?
4. How will this help others?

Questions on Customer Satisfaction for Achieving Excellent Customer Performance
1. How will a satisfied or happy client describe your business?
2. How will you improve customer satisfaction by creating a higher purpose for your business?

3. How will you apply your business core values in creating higher customer satisfaction?
4. How will you expand this concept to your community, business associates, and co-workers?
5. What will you do in your business to help expand and promote this consciousness?

These questions guide the client to create or recreate a mission, vision, and core values for the company. This impacts the culture of the organization. Additionally, it creates and defines a deeper and meaningful purpose.

> *"How will you apply your business core values in creating higher customer satisfaction?"*

VISION BOARDS ARE VALUABLE WHEN APPLYING SPIRITUAL INTELLIGENCE

Another tool to help your client connect to spiritual intelligence is by creating a vision board. Many prosperous and successful business people create a vision board to manifest their goals. A vision board is a tool your client artistically creates to solidify their goals through pictures, collages, and positive affirmation statements. You can define your hopes, goals, visions, and dreams on this board. Vision boards are meant for exploring and creating the limitless possibilities in your personal and professional lives. It becomes a powerful visualization tool for you to create and manifest your utmost desires. The purpose of the vision board is to activate the concept of the law of attraction. The law of attraction simply means that you attract things into your life based upon how you think. If you think positively, you will attract positive energy. If you begin to think about success, you will attract success. Conversely, if you think negatively, that will be the energy you are drawing into your life and business. The creation of a vision board attracts positive energy into one's life and manifests what an individual wants to accomplish. While preparing your vision board, you must think big and think outside of the box. By creating a vision board, you are applying spiritual intelligence and connecting to a higher source to help manifest the individual's biggest dreams.

Personally, I created a vision dream board in the early 1980's. Recently, when I was spring cleaning, I rediscovered the board. Everything on my vision board has manifested in my life. The board detailed aspects of my personal and professional lives. When I looked at the vision board, I realized my thinking at that time was limited and I did not explore the limitless possibilities. So, I have now applied spiritual intelligence and created a new, expansive vision board. It explores limitless aspects of my life and all the dreams I want to manifest. Recommending a client to create a vision board containing positive affirmations can create a more concrete method to allow the client to connect to his or her spiritual intelligence, and create the life they only once dreamed about.

The creation of the vision board allows the client to utilize the client's right side of the brain, the creative and imaginative energy. This creates an opening for the client's spiritual energy, SQ, to flow. The client can go beyond his or her own personal limitations by creating a vision board. Expression and creativity is through one's free will. There are no guidelines, structure or rules that create confinements in one's freedom of expression. In essence, you are allowing a client's spirit to soar and be fully expressed in the physical format. This is one tool a client can create to help achieve personal growth, prosperity, and success.

WHAT ARE THE BENEFITS OF SPIRITUAL INTELLIGENCE IN BUSINESS?

There are many benefits to the client from coaching him or her to apply spiritual intelligence. As mentioned, the client can begin to search for a deeper meaning in business. This will begin to activate characteristics of empathy and compassion for co-workers, colleagues, and customers. It can also enhance the client's self-esteem and provide the client with a stronger sense of identity. This will then assist the client in becoming more confident and comfortable in the workplace. It creates stronger working relationships amongst colleagues, co-workers, and management. Team building and leadership strengthens one's business and fosters growth. The building of more empathetic and compassionate relationships in the workplace creates stability and improves morale. This ultimately enhances customer satisfaction and profitability.

> *"A company creates a strong structure by seeking a deeper meaning in the company's true purpose through exploring the soul intelligence."*

If your client is the owner, a shareholder, or a leader of the company, you can coach the client to build a strong organizational culture. A company creates a strong structure by seeking a deeper meaning in the company's true purpose through exploring the soul intelligence. Employees who seek more spiritual awareness become more positive. This builds morale and team spirit, and decreases turnover. Positive-minded individuals are also less likely to become ill so there is a decrease in absenteeism. Additionally, they become more positively motivated which increases their performance and productivity at work. Further, it enhances their creative energy which allows them to think outside of the box and apply more creativity in problem solving. New and innovative ideas can be inspired by applying spiritual intelligence at the client's company.

Spiritual intelligence in building a business allows the leader to lead with a stronger vision, core values, and a more meaningful purpose which creates a stronger culture for the company. The employees have a greater sense of identity, self-esteem, and self-worth. This ultimately creates a workplace where the employees make better choices. Better choices create a better business. The employee feels they are more connected to the company. The more connected the employee feels, the greater the sense of satisfaction. Ultimately this will flow through the corporate structure.

> *"Spiritual intelligence in building a business allows the leader to lead with a stronger vision, core values, and a more meaningful purpose which creates a stronger culture for the company."*

HOW TO ACTIVATE SPIRITUAL INTELLIGENCE BY SERVING THE COMMUNITY

When the client applies spiritual intelligence in their personal and business life, an inner voice becomes a guiding light, a door opens to the connection to one's higher source. The client begins to take responsibility for his or her words, thoughts, and actions which can ultimately empower the client to be more in control of the client's destiny. Once people begin to understand at some level that they are the cause of their actions, people will begin to behave and act in a different manner. People will begin to treat others with more human dignity and respect. It brings a new level to the meaning of love thy neighbor as thyself.

One principle of spiritual intelligence is to begin to act selflessly and replace the 'me' selfish consciousness with the 'we' consciousness. When we do so, we realize our true life's purpose is to help others. We begin to see a critical change in how we treat our fellow human beings. There are many for-profit and not-for-profit organizations that follow this concept. Spirituality for Kids International, Inc. (SFK), a not-for-profit educational organization (http://www.spiritualityforkids.com), provides an interactive children's learning program that helps create and teach awareness of universal spiritual laws and principles. The ultimate goal is for a child to achieve self-fulfillment and behave in a proactive manner. One exercise taught in a SFK class is called 'sharing the flame.' In this simple exercise, each child is given a candle. One candle is lit and the children begin to share the flame in a dark room. As the flame is passed, the room becomes illuminated and the light emerges. The room is fully lit and the darkness has disappeared. The children realize it all began with the light of one candle that was shared, candle by candle. This simple exercise embraces the power of sharing and how through one consistent simple act we can create a room of light with unity.

This simple lesson exemplifies the concept of service to others, which is another principle of spiritual intelligence. By providing excellent and high quality service to your customers or client base, you elevate your business to the next level. If we perceive our life purpose is to help others by assisting them mentally and emotionally, we have created and activated a universal principle. We can expand this concept by giving back to others and our community.

The coach can ask the client the following questions:
1. Where and how do you volunteer your time?
2. How does volunteering make you feel?
3. How will you help grow this feeling in your community?
4. What not-for-profits does your business support?
5. How do you and your co-workers feel in supporting them?
6. How will you help other businesses support not-for-profits in your community?

This mindset encourages community service. It shifts your actions and thoughts to thinking about mankind. This expands the sense of consciousness, opening the door to limitless possibilities.

THE REASONS, THE WHAT, AND THE HOW

Coaching a client to reaching his or her highest potential can be successfully achieved by applying spiritual intelligence. As a coach, you apply the questions from The Reasons, The What, and The How to invoke the deepest meaning. It is your inner voice that is the driving force to accomplish transformative personal and professional growth, which in turn empowers a client to achieve and accomplish goals beyond his or her own limitations and expectations.

The client will begin to explore and find a deeper meaning in life. The door opens for the client to explore and expand their creativity and break through personal barriers. Actions of compassion, sharing, and empathy emerge in the client's work environment. A shift begins and expansive thought enlightens and broadens the workplace. Unity emerges and the business organization strengthens. Applying universal laws and connecting the client's spiritual intelligence will create a global change in the client's consciousness, eventually creating the positive energy of transformation, which will help improve the global consciousness for mankind.

Wendy is CEO and Founder of RecreatingU, an executive coaching and consulting company. As an excellence coach, she focuses on clients seeking to achieve a more meaningful life. She applies spiritual intelligence in her practice so her clients explore and develop a stronger purpose in their lives. This creates a new awareness for clients to achieve their excellence.

Wendy continues to study spirituality as she has for the past twenty-five years. Through her studies, she explores many aspects of personal growth. By applying spiritual intelligence in her practice, her clients begin to explore a deeper meaning to personal and professional development. Wendy is also an active global board member of Spirituality for Kids. SFK is an educational not for profit that teaches children how to apply universal and spiritual consciousness in their daily lives.

Wendy is co-managing partner of Glantzlaw, a multi-discipline law firm in South Florida. She has practiced complex family law litigation, as well as lectured and authored on many aspects of family law. She is a Florida Family Law Certified Mediator.

Her mission is to combine her spiritual and business acumen in coaching her clients in achieving their excellence. Her vision is to help create a global change in the consciousness of each person by awaking human dignity and respect.

IT ALL ADDS UP – ADD/ADHD COACHING FOR TEENS
by Gina M. Wilson

Teenagers today are faced with challenges and opportunities different from as little as ten years ago, largely due to 'the connected world' – mobile connectivity and ready availability of information through the internet and Smartphones. A 2012 Pew Research Institute survey showed internet access among American teens has changed dramatically, citing that a staggering 95% use the internet, 37% of teens own Smartphones, and 23% have a tablet computer. Distractions are ever-present even for the most focused and disciplined individual of any age.

For a teenager who has Attention Deficit Disorder (ADD), normal hormonal changes of adolescence exacerbate the symptoms of ADD. Diminished self-esteem and an increase in risk behaviors are common. Many parents find that once a child with ADD becomes a teenager, the challenges of ADD become much greater and the teen may actually lose ground in areas where he or she had been successful before as a child. Grades fall, assignments get lost or forgotten, personal items get misplaced, social relationships are affected, and automobile accidents occur at a higher rate than for non-ADD teens.

These challenges create a demand for professionals who understand, and a specific market has emerged for ADD coaches. Coaching provides a means for individuals with ADD to overcome the challenges presented by creating awareness and identifying strategies that can be used to attain personal goals. Indeed, many of the techniques used in ADD coaching, including those described in this chapter, can be applied in coaching other populations as well. ADD coaching is extremely fulfilling and rewarding for the coach who can facilitate the personal, academic, and social empowerment of these individuals. While those with ADD/ADHD have specific common challenges, the range of abilities and talent among the group is great. Coaches must recognize that each individual is unique and work with them to define and develop their own strategies for success. Many teens with ADD are high-performers, highly intelligent, and gifted. ADD is not in itself a determinant of future success in life, and must be considered in relation to the whole person. I have found that coaching the whole-person, exploring the wider picture of goals, challenges and circumstances, rather than coaching for only the ADD factor, is more effective for these clients. If poorly managed, the challenges ADD presents can become obstacles to achieving personal success. ADD coaches create awareness and help the client recognize how it manifests itself for them. Coaching helps the client learn to re-frame a situation in a positive light regardless of the presence of ADD. An important role of the ADD coach is to work with the client to develop coping

"Many teens with ADD are high-performers, highly intelligent, and gifted."

mechanisms and techniques for successful management of symptoms.

The same guidelines for successful coaching apply to coaching ADD teens, and there are some which are particularly important that are discussed throughout this chapter:

- Communicate clearly: Be specific and consistent with explanations, action steps, and expectations.
- Maintain a regular schedule.
- Minimize distractions.
- Encourage the teen to engage in activities with opportunities for success.
- Continually reference affirmations and recognize positive language and behaviors to build self-esteem.
- Provide specific alternatives for organization and time management.
- Encourage healthy living through exploration of health, social, academic, and spiritual goals, and discuss healthy behaviors.
- Encourage ownership of feelings and behavior; discourage blaming and 'poor me' attitudes.

WHAT IS ADD/ADHD EXACTLY?

There are many misconceptions about ADD and it is important for the coach to understand the facts in order to create empathy and develop an accurate awareness for the client. According to the Diagnostic and Statistical Manual of Mental Disorders, (DSM-IV), considered the foremost reference used by clinicians and researchers to diagnose and classify mental health disorders, Attention Deficit Hyperactivity Disorder or AD/HD is characterized by the pervasive presence of distractibility, impulsivity, and inattention in multiple settings over an extended period of time.

"Continually reference affirmations and recognize positive language and behaviors to build self-esteem."

DSM-IV cites those with AD/HD exhibit several characteristics such as inattention, making careless mistakes, appearing as not listening, struggles with following directions, forgetfulness, restlessness, excessive physical activity, talking excessively, losing things, interrupting, impatience, and challenges with staying focused or following directions.

Note that degree and frequency of exhibited behaviors are important factors in the diagnosis of ADHD. Occasional occurrences of the above behavior does not warrant an ADHD diagnosis, and indeed, circumstances such as sleep deprivation, experiencing a traumatic event, or presence of another mental disorder such as schizophrenia, for example, can elicit similar behavior in persons without ADHD.

Although DSM-IV defined three subtypes, the somewhat

controversial and newly-published DSM-5 (May, 2013) has eliminated classification of subtypes, citing research over the last 20 years demonstrating that symptoms are less exclusive than originally thought, meaning that those with ADD/ADHD are likely to exhibit various degrees of both inattention and hyperactivity, which may vary over a lifetime. In addition, the DSM-5 includes more criteria for diagnosing adults. Other than clinicians, however, most people (including this author) use the generic term 'ADD' for describing both the ADHD and ADD conditions. While many people exhibit occasional symptoms of ADD, the clinical diagnosis of ADD must be done by a licensed healthcare professional. The clinician will rule out other medical or mental health conditions, or temporary situations which could be responsible for symptoms, and determine if DSM criteria are met.

ADD is recognized by the Federal Government as a disability, and individuals with ADD are protected under the Americans with Disabilities Act and the Individuals with Disabilities Education Act. This legislation enables those with ADD to obtain appropriate and reasonable accommodations in schools and in employment settings, which help to increase efficiency and productivity. School accommodations may include offerings such as extended time for examinations, priority classroom seating, distraction-free locations for examinations, or audio textbooks. Accommodations are unique to an individual and can be obtained when the family provides the required, extensive documentation of clinical diagnosis, healthcare records, and recommendations from the student's care team. Some people with ADD require no accommodations at all.

- The National Center for Health Statistics reports that for 2012, 8.4% of children ages 3-17 have been diagnosed with ADHD.
- Boys are two times more likely than girls to be diagnosed.
- The condition is not out-grown.
- ADD impacts school, work, family, and social relationships.
- ADD may co-exist with other conditions.
- Symptoms are pervasive and persist over a long period of time.

Many teens with ADD have been diagnosed in early elementary school years. Since diagnosis relies heavily on reports from parents and teachers, observation by professionals, and qualitative data, a diagnosis can be elusive and is often confounded by the presence of other medical or mental health conditions. Unfortunately, many people have misconceptions about the cause of ADD. It is *not* a result of poor parenting, family situation, food allergies, sugar intake, or brain injury. Research shows that although other factors may contribute to ADD symptoms, scientists generally agree that ADD is caused by biological factors which alter the activity of neurotransmitters in the brain, and there is also strong support for genetic influence. Families with one member diagnosed have a 25-35% chance of having another family member diagnosed with ADD, whereas for the general population, the likelihood is 5-6%.

Teens with ADD may or may not take medication for it. Healthcare professionals generally recognize the most effective treatment for ADD to be a combination of medication, counseling or behavior therapy, and, increasingly, coaching to improve organization skills and productivity, and build self-esteem. There are also naturopathic and alternative treatments. Cognitive or behavioral therapy fosters behavior modification and modifies thought patterns and the emotional effects of living with ADD (NIMH.gov). Medications typically prescribed for ADHD (stimulants or non-stimulants) have long been established as safe for use in pediatric and adolescent populations. Despite this, many parents are reluctant to allow their teen to use medication as a treatment for ADHD, citing side effects, religious reasons, social stigma, and prohibitive costs as reasons not to medicate.

In my personal experience as a parent of two ADD young adults, and as a Coach for students and adults with ADD, I consider the name ADD/ADHD misleading. Rather than attention *deficit*, the condition might be more appropriately named 'ARD' – attention *regulation* disorder. Ask any parent of a teen with ADD and they can cite examples of times when their teen had absolutely no trouble attending to a favorite TV show or focusing on a project which they enjoyed doing. Rather than an absolute *inability* to focus, it may be that the teen has trouble *adjusting* focus from one activity to another, focusing on an unpleasant task, or completing an undesired chore. Pervasive inattentiveness may be relatively easy to diagnose; consider also the teen who is hyper-focused when building a model and yet unable to focus long enough to read the biology chapter of his textbook. Increasingly, healthcare professionals are recognizing the inability to *adjust or change* focus as a symptom of ADD.

> *"Rather than an absolute inability to focus, it may be that the teen has trouble adjusting focus..."*

TEAMING WITH HEALTH CARE AND MENTAL HEALTH PROFESSIONALS

As mentioned earlier, clinicians generally agree that the most effective treatment for teens with ADD is a multi-faceted approach among various providers. Not all of the treatment modalities are appropriate for everyone with ADD, yet many people with ADD have a team of support providers who together address their various needs. The coach clearly communicates to the client at the onset that the coach does not (and is not licensed to) provide medical, psychological, or counseling services, and instead offers a means for clients to overcome challenges, explore opportunities, and develop action plans.

Parents often first consult the child's pediatrician if they suspect ADHD, or the physician initiates discussions with parents based on observations during medical visits. Alternatively, a teacher may alert parents to problem behaviors exhibited in the classroom. Regardless of how the query is initiated, once a person is diagnosed, the diagnostician often recommends a team of professionals with specialized knowledge, or the family seeks support independently. While a family doctor may have been the first point of contact, a specialist may ultimately be responsible for the medical care. Only a physician can legally prescribe medication, determine the best product and dosage, and monitor side effects. Some ADD patients see a neurologist or psychiatrist depending on the presence of other conditions. A therapist often provides psychological support. Coaches augment the team by supporting the client in exploring options, defining goals, overcoming challenges presented by the ADD condition, and moving toward achieving goals. The coach may consult with the other providers only if the client has authorized sharing of his/her health information with the coach through the use of a legal document (the healthcare provider's HIPAA documentation).

> *"Coaches augment the team by supporting the client in exploring options, defining goals, overcoming challenges presented by the ADD condition, and moving toward achieving goals."*

COACHING CHALLENGES WITH THIS POPULATION

In my coaching practice, I require a Sponsored Coaching engagement for any adolescent client who is under age 18. A sponsored coaching engagement involves a third party who is responsible for the financial and legal aspects of the coaching contract, and the third party engages the coach to work with the client. The adolescent is the client; the engagement involves both client and sponsor. Typically the sponsor is one or both parents, grandparents, or a legal guardian. Teens in foster care may be sponsored by the state or their foster parents.

Sponsored Coaching is more effective for minors for several reasons. Maturity level is a significant factor that greatly impacts autonomy and the ability to make decisions and execute an action plan. Sponsors help support the teen and facilitate their action plans through encouragement, monetary support, material support, and sustained guidance. The Sponsored Coaching engagement utilizes the sponsor both as the person who signs the agreement and as the party responsible for payment, then also as an active, regular participant in the coaching process. It is important to keep the sponsor informed about the progress of coaching sessions with client permission. As with other forms of coaching, such as an employee / employer-sponsored engagement, the ADD coach's challenge is to maintain client confidentiality while simultaneously keeping the sponsor informed and involved. I achieve this through providing the sponsor with regular summary reports after obtaining approval from the client. Thus the sponsor is copied on action plans set by the client, and involved in overcoming obstacles when appropriate. This empowers me to share appropriate information while protecting the confidentiality agreement and developing trust. Upon receipt of the Summary Report, the sponsor may provide feedback and insight. I then provide this perspective in the next session with the client and solicit their reaction. This sometimes presents a delicate balance for the coach to reconcile the sponsor's desired outcome and the client's stated objectives. Disparity creates a great opportunity to explore differences and frequently generates valuable insights.

> *"Reports to the sponsor must first be approved by the client."*

For the coach, sponsored coaching engagements are nearly double the work. Communications must occur with both client and sponsor individually. Reports to the sponsor must first be approved by the client. Frequently there are competing agendas from client and sponsor, and on occasion the coach must conduct a session with both together to ensure that all are aware of the goals each has set. This joint session is also used to clarify priorities. At other times, regular family coaching (in which the teen, their sponsor, and possibly other family members participate in the sessions) may be appropriate for the

ADD teen and their sponsor, and the coach may recommend this if competing agendas persist or if deemed appropriate based on the teen's maturity level. When initiating the engagement, a coach and their client may discuss this approach as an alternative.

OOPS! WE HAD AN APPOINTMENT?

Scheduling appointments is particularly daunting in today's busy families. Families have varied schedules based on age of the children and their school calendar, whether or not both parents work outside the home, presence of siblings, participation in varsity sports or travel teams, part-time jobs or volunteer commitments, and the myriad lessons, groups, and activities of today's students. Fitting in regular coaching sessions is challenging for some families to work into their already overcrowded schedules. Considering the regularity of school hours from Monday through Friday, coaching teens may involve weekend or evening appointments. Early risers may prefer the morning hours before school starts, as this can be the only 'untapped' time in their calendar. When I first started coaching ADD teens, I often did not schedule the next sessions until the end of each session, in an effort to remain flexible for the client. I soon learned that a) teens are often not in complete control of their calendar, as they often expected to run everything by Mom or Dad to ensure no conflict with the family calendar, b) the teens I coached were likely to go along with any suggested time without considering other happenings, only to reschedule at the last minute, and c) time management is a challenge for ADD clients (and families) and often one of the challenges they are looking to overcome through coaching.

Rescheduled appointments and 'no shows' are problematic. I have incorporated the following scheduling techniques and, in doing so, have mitigated scheduling issues and averted logistical obstacles:

- Create a tentative schedule that both sponsor and client agree upon for the first four sessions, when the coaching agreement is signed. Towards the end of these four, establish the next four, etc.
- With each follow-up email to the client, include a reminder of the schedule for the next few sessions, and ask for confirmation of these dates and times.
- Collect alternate phone numbers for client and sponsor in the event of a late or missed appointment.
- Utilize text messaging to notify the teen the day of the appointment and remind them of their scheduled time. (Teens love texting!) It is also a good idea to text the sponsor as well because they can help facilitate punctuality.
- Whenever possible, establish a regular day of the week and time for the coaching sessions. Regularity facilitates time management, decreases risk of cancellations, and reinforces the client's and sponsor's commitment to coaching.

The coach facilitates scheduling and helps clients keep their commitment through modeling positive and effective techniques for time management and follow-through, which clients can incorporate into their own time management skills.

A unique challenge with teens is the ebb and flow of school schedules. There are periods of intense schoolwork during exams, weeks of erratic sports schedules during championships, occasional field trips, and holiday vacations. Typically, I avoid scheduling sessions with teen clients during these times rather than trying to work around tentative or contingent schedules. Some clients do take advantage of school vacation days to fit in a session and of course this is a great opportunity for quality session time if it works for the student.

DIGITAL DIVIDE

While many teens are heavy users of cell phones, iTunes, YouTube, Facebook, Instagram, and Pinterest, surprisingly few use the myriad apps available nowadays for addressing the perhaps more mundane and pragmatic issues of daily life. For example, most of my student ADD clients were not using any form of computer calendar/planner such as Outlook, iCal, or Google Calendar at the beginning of the coaching engagement. The 'great digital divide', a term commonly used to describe the widening gap of access to technology among various socioeconomic groups, may also aptly describe the narrow spectrum of apps used by the teen demographic. Even generational differences between Generation X (those born 1960 – 1980) and the later Millenials (born 1981- 2000) exist in terms of the *kinds* of apps they are using, particularly when it comes to productivity tools versus entertainment or content apps. For teens with ADD, technology can be their best friend.

A significant component of coaching ADD clients is often the exploration of various digital tools and apps to improve organizational and time management skills. The coach must be able to comfortably discuss various tools so that a client can choose among several alternatives to find the ones which best suit their style. While posing a continual challenge for the coach, staying ahead of the latest app craze is important for relevancy in today's world and for enhancing rapport with teens. Readily available, and requiring little new financial investment, some 'must-have' tools for ADDers (and others) to consider using are:

> *"...staying ahead of the latest app craze is important for relevancy in today's world and for enhancing rapport with teens."*

- Smartphone Voice Recorder App
- Smartphone calendar for appointments, reminders, alarms
- Skype, FaceTime, or Hangouts for group projects/discussions

- Calendar sharing (laptop or phone) with family members
- Using headphones to block out distracting sounds (with or without music, there are Apps for white noise, nature sounds)
- Timely reminders on the computer to periodically remind the user to get up and take a break (from homework, studying)
- Sticky Notes and similar apps to replace all those paper notes and 'to do' lists
- Syncing computer, tablet, and cell phone so your 'stuff' is current on all devices
- Using SkyDrive, Drop Box, Google Docs or other cloud services for portability of documents
- Shared contacts list among various Email accounts
- Using Spellchecker and Grammar check features in composing documents
- Scheduling computer back-ups to the cloud (or external hard drive) to prevent loss of schoolwork and other important content

Paradoxically, frustration with chosen technology often contributes to clients' stress. Poor organization skills are exacerbated by a messy computer 'desktop'. Having hundreds of icons to choose from, finding a document misfiled upon download, and other such nuisances are maddening and often stressful. While the computer often mandates attention to detail, the ADDer is prone to careless errors. Following instructions is often a challenge for ADDers while installation of any new app or download requires a series of exact steps to be followed. Understandably, technology can be the double-edged sword for someone with ADD.

PACE AND FORMAT

As a coach, we are taught to move at the client's pace, matching their style in the moment and echoing their words and ideas. In coaching a teenager with ADD, the client's pace of communication is often erratic, easily interrupted by distracting thoughts or sounds. While every coaching session begins with a reminder to be in a quiet, distraction-free environment, ADDers must deal with noise in their own mind – the distracting, random, racing thoughts so common among those with ADD. Regardless of how ideal the physical environment, or how physically still the client appears, an ADD client may experience distractions which are imperceptible to the coach. The coach must continually re-focus the discussion to the topic at hand and reel in the client as appropriate.

> *"As a coach, we are taught to move at the client's pace, matching their style in the moment and echoing their words and ideas."*

Some clients actually concentrate better when they are *not* still. There are clients who prefer to doodle, tap their fingers, rock in a rocking chair, or listen to music at a low volume during a coaching session. This 'sidebar' activity often increases the client's focus and ability to attend more closely to the interchange with the coach. One of the coach's roles is to help the client establish early on what is most comfortable and effective for them, and even help them discover the potential of having a sidebar activity. In some cases, the client has already discovered this for themselves or through counseling; often this is discovered within the coaching process itself and is a considerable milestone for both client and coach. While traditional educational environments often discourage extraneous movement or sounds, there is value for some students in having sidebar activities. I have seen with my own children that although at times they were seemingly disengaged (at the computer or playing a game) they were able to recite, nearly verbatim, the whole of a conversation being held around them. A benefit of ADD for some is the ability to multi-task!

Interrupting others or finishing others' sentences before they have finished are common characteristics with ADD. The coach must recognize this and with compassion and patience encourage the client with a gentle 'please let me finish'. In addition, the client may jump to answer questions with a quick 'I don't know' or simple answer. Circumvent this by encouraging the client to take their time by saying, "Take a few minutes to think about (whatever the question is), maybe even jot it down, before you answer" or ,"Tell me more."

The coach may find repeating the question to elicit more of a response and focus attention useful. Conversely, the client may at times speak at such a fast pace that the ideas are disconnected and the speech is slurred or incoherent. I have frequently asked clients to repeat or re-state a response to help me understand which also serves to help them articulate and clarify their own thoughts. For some clients, I incorporate a quick stress management exercise at the beginning of a session as a means of regulating pace and fostering clarity.

The coaching session may sometimes feel disjointed. The coach must work to keep the teen on track and moving forward, reigning in the conversation when the teen moves off on unrelated tangents. Frequent re-statement of goals and action steps keeps those thoughts in the forefront. The affirmation and affirmation statements are powerful tools that facilitate maintaining focus on desired states and ideally are referenced frequently. To minimize rambling, the coach may enforce a time limit for session questions, or ask quantitative questions, i.e. "What are your three biggest obstacles…?"

> *"The affirmation and affirmation statements are powerful tools that facilitate maintaining focus on desired states …"*

TIME MANAGEMENT

As we saw earlier in this chapter, losing or forgetting important things is a common challenge for those with ADD. Losing track of time, missing assignments or appointments, and managing schoolwork are all repeatedly noted by many teen ADD clients as challenges they want to overcome. Sponsors for these clients similarly identify time management and organization skills as those areas particularly troublesome for their teens. Teens themselves cite both lack of time and disorganization as obstacles to achieving their goals (such as maintaining a high grade point average, gaining college admission, or good relationship with parents). Regardless of the goal, the coach, through modeling time management skills and holding the client accountable for action steps, continually reinforces the value of time management. Time management is a learned skill, and most students are not faced with time management issues until they become more autonomous or face problems resulting from poor time management. For teens particularly, whose time is largely controlled by parents, autonomy comes only after they have demonstrated that can effectively manage homework, extra-curricular activities, TV, and commitments.

> *"Time management is a learned skill..."*

WHAT DOES THIS MEAN FOR COACHES?

While not directly part of the coaching process, the coach can be contracted independently by the sponsor as a consultant to teach time management skills. The sponsor may also have time management challenges, and if the sponsor forgets the coaching session, the teen may have a schedule conflict. As noted earlier, it is wise to include the sponsor on all reminders and appointment scheduling, as teens are subject to the family schedule. Disorganized families can inadvertently sabotage a teen's successful time management due to interdependencies.

THE PARENT AS SPONSOR

Perhaps one of the most challenging issues related to coaching ADD teens is managing the sponsor relationship during the coaching engagement. Since ADD tends to run in families, there is a good probability that the sponsor, if he or she is the biological parent, also has ADD, yet he or she is not the client. They may face many of the same challenges as their teen, and may or may not be successfully managing their ADD. Many of the techniques for working with ADD teens can also be used when communicating with the sponsor.

It is important to note that prior to 1980, when the DSM III introduced the terminology ADD, the condition was poorly understood and widely controversial among clinicians and laypersons, resulting in a significantly lower rate of diagnosis than today. This left many people undiagnosed or unfortunately labeled disparagingly out of societal ignorance and misconception. So, while genetic factors increase the likelihood of ADD in families, parents and older siblings may not have been officially diagnosed. It is also common that even after being diagnosed, families themselves are not fully informed. Sensitivity, compassion, and respectful interaction with everyone improves the coach's rapport with the family.

In conclusion, coaching teenage ADD clients is both challenging and rewarding. A successful coach will understand that having ADD is just one facet of a person, and will utilize specific techniques and whole-person coaching skills to empower these individuals to achieve their full potential and realize their dreams. Coaching can be the successful vehicle for self-awareness, positive self-esteem, and the development of specific techniques for both managing and embracing ADD!

"Coaching can be the successful vehicle for self-awareness, positive self-esteem, and the development of specific techniques for both managing and embracing ADD!"

Gina Wilson, MS, CEO of Empowerment Strategies, has over 25 years' experience as a management consultant, business owner, speaker, college instructor, and software developer. Gina offers Executive / Career, ADD /ADHD, College Admissions, and Life Transitions coaching. Gina is Founder and Principal Consultant of System Strategies, a consulting firm specializing in healthcare IT.

Gina's interest in coaching stems from a lifelong fascination with human thought, behavior, health, and wellness. With a Master of Science in Cognitive Psychology from Villanova, and a Certified Professional Coach, Gina brings a unique perspective to coaching. She taught psychology at Villanova University and Delaware Technical and Community College, and has spoken for the University of Pennsylvania, Duke, Villanova, at conferences, and community groups. A parent of children with ADD/ADHD, Gina is keenly aware of the challenges and opportunities. She promotes awareness, knowledge, and empathy within education, the workplace, and communities.

Her vision is a world where people are empowered to thrive and develop to their full potential through recognition, expression, development, and celebration of unique individual talents.

www.Empowerment-Strategies.com

Your Career Narrative is a Story That Works
by Brian Beatty

If I were to ask about your work, you will tell me a story of sorts. You won't stop to prepare it, because you know it well, you tell it all the time. Usually in bits and pieces. To friends and colleagues. With clients. Sometimes in a key interview. Even though you may not realize it, and even if you don't fully own it, this is your Career Narrative.

Most of us have faced challenges in our careers. Most of us are well aware of the pressure to sell ourselves – and far too many of us dread it. Dress it up as marketing, improve your presentation, work on your personal brand, and what's the bottom line? Like it or not, you're still selling yourself. The question is, how to do it?

Here's a proven, effective solution: present your career as a great story.

In this chapter we will explore how rethinking and reworking your Career Narrative can be the ideal means of presenting, leveraging, and marketing your strengths and accomplishments. The rewards are drawn from scientific studies, as well as the ancient power of narrative, with direct benefits gained from a wide-ranging approach informed by personal branding and the collapse of traditional narratives in the digital era.

YOU ARE ALREADY TELLING THE STORY OF YOUR CAREER

Your Career Narrative is much more than your education, your profession, and your resume. It involves your work history, in an individual series of events unlike anyone else's. It pivots on critical choices, and progresses with key interests, which amount to much more than what you've achieved – it tips us off to the depth and breadth of all you have to offer. Career Narrative even allows us a glimpse into the unique essence of who you are, and that's just the beginning. There's more, and it is unfolding right now. Yours is quite a story.

> *"Career Narrative even allows us a glimpse into the unique essence of who you are, and that's just the beginning."*

If you're communicating this important history without knowing you're telling a story, the chances are you've lost control of the message, and you're underappreciated, if not misunderstood. Perhaps you're struggling in your career. Or miss-communicating with your boss. Or blowing the deal with a client. Have you ever fumbled a job interview? Well they just weren't buying your story. Or your work. Or you.

If you're in the habit of presenting yourself with self-deprecating humor or self-effacing modesty, and your competition has mastered the art of self-promotion by telling his compelling story, who wins?

Your narrative determines the way people evaluate and respond to you. The focus with my clients is simple: *tell a better story*. In other words, redefine yourself, and tell us all about it. It really is a great story! Tell your story simply; tell it on your terms. Find your voice, and perfect it, so you hold their interest. Tell them a story where the outcome is your success. Who doesn't love a happy ending?

MAKE YOUR STORIES PERSUASIVE

Think about the last time you heard a good story. And then? ... What happens next? ... Storytelling restores our sense of discovery, and keeps us in touch with possibilities. That's because the format of a narrative, where events unfold one after the other, have a profound impact on our imagination. There's leverage in discovery. Possibilities open up. The future unfolds anew. You find yourself in a liberating way.

Have you ever told a friend a story and then two weeks later, he mentions the same thing, as if it was *his* idea? According to research from Princeton, storytelling is the surest way to plant an idea into someone's mind. It activates the brain so that a listener can turn the narrative into *his own* idea and experience. This is one of the most powerful means of winning people over, and it's been happening for centuries.

> *"...storytelling is the surest way to plant an idea..."*

Stories are persuasive, and they drive action. They're constructed with a plot and based on actions steps, and that is their potential leverage – to inspire further actions. Narrative works.

> *"Stories are persuasive, and they drive action."*

Imagine this: we're sitting around a campfire devouring a delicious meal – fresh fish, just caught in a nearby lake. I tell you how I caught them earlier in the day. I'm excited, it's fresh in my mind, the details are lining up, from the time of day, where I fished, the bait I used, my technique, and how I reeled them in. On the story goes, full of vivid details leading to the happy ending, which happens to be the mouth-watering meal on a plate before us.

I could ask you if you wanted more fish and you would probably say yes. I might invite you to go fishing with me, and again you would be inclined to say yes. I could offer to show you how I do it, and yet again, *yes*.

The power of persuasion can inform every story you tell. You already tell stories, so imbue them with more purpose and greater power. I've helped many clients redefine their narratives, and you too can present your career as a compelling story.

WE ARE ALL WIRED FOR STORYTELLING

I just love a good story, who doesn't? And I'm not alone. As it turns out, our brains are designed for stories, and neuroscience has been very busy proving it. Researchers have known for some time that certain regions of the brain are involved in how we interpret written words. More recently the buzz is about how narratives activate many other parts of our brains as well – that's why the experience of getting lost in a story can feel so real.

Yes, we're *wired* for storytelling, and we activate our brains more efficiently when we listen to a story. Stories, when reduced to their simplest form, connect cause and effect. That's fundamentally how we think – in narratives, all day long, we make up quick stories in our heads for every action and conversation.

> *"Yes, we're wired for storytelling, and we activate our brains more efficiently when we l isten to a s tory."*

Tell a story and your brain will synchronize with the brains of your listeners. We've been evolving that way for thousands of years; before we could write them down, the beliefs, values, and behavioral codes of humankind were passed down through stories. *Shh*, listen... you can hear them around the fire. Stories were essential for our survival and success as an evolving species, and their effect is thriving today, as your potential.

And storytelling can be tapped for your benefit, or perhaps the very survival of your career.

OVERCOMING OBSTACLES IS UNIVERSAL

In his groundbreaking study of myth, Joseph Campbell presented a universal tale of how we prevail in the face of seemingly insurmountable obstacles. He used James Joyce's term, calling it the monomyth. It's a hero's journey. Campbell asserted that major stories and myths from a broad range of times and places share basic universal structures. In various books, documentaries, and films, he made a compelling case for how we all benefit, individually and across cultures, from this mythical journey. The television series he made with Billy Moyers was a watershed in public broadcasting and its impact on popular culture.

Monomyths influenced countless artists, musicians, poets, and filmmakers. Chief among them is Lucas, who acknowledged Campbell's influence in both the original *Star Wars* trilogy and its prequels. The structure of the narrative arc of Campbell's hero's journey can be essentially boiled down to this: "*the hero comes back from this adventure with the power to bestow boons on his fellow man."* What a powerful definition of career potential!

The same essential story applies to your career path. You've worked hard to get this far, you've prepared, studied, faced challenges, overcome the odds, and you have a lot to offer. The question is, do they know it? Have you told them? *Can* you tell them? We're talking about your boss, when it's time for your performance review, or the person sitting across from you at a job interview, or perhaps your clients.

The ancient tradition of storytelling corroborates scientific studies. Together they build a strong argument for telling a compelling story of your career.

BENEFIT FROM THE COLLAPSE OF NARRATIVE IN THE DIGITAL AGE

We seem hard-wired to the present, especially when it comes to our work. Everything is streaming live, in real time, and it just keeps going. Email is being replaced by texting, blogs are outdated as soon as they're posted, hence the Twitter feeds. Polished scripts are too slow to write and too labor-intensive, so there's reality television. Long-term investment and interest-bearing currency are running out of capital as the markets chase ever more mysterious financial products. Facebook and YouTube lead the charge in breaking news before CNN arrives.

In his thought-provoking book, *Present Shock,* Douglas Rushkoff underscores all of the above and more. In the first chapter entitled *Narrative Collapse*, he perceptively points out that we no longer have time to even acknowledge, let alone embody the big, overarching narratives that our values, beliefs, and culture are based on. It's even truer in presentations and marketing online; it's not so much about the product, it's all in the immediate experience. In other words, if you're not the customer, you're the product. He's exaggerating, of course, to sell books, and yet it's easy to see how this overwhelming new reality can actually work in our favor.

Which leads to a problem: if we live in the digital now, and we have short attention spans, and our competition is everywhere online, we *really* are pushed to quicken our strategies and condense our narratives. *I've got a minute, what's your story?* In reality, it's not even a minute. The window of opportunity to engage is, on the average, less than 30 seconds.

I've designed an exercise for clients when they feel stuck and at a loss for words in how to present their careers. First, print your resume. Then stand before a mirror and read every word aloud (I didn't say that this was a *fun* exercise). Hear it as if it were new to you, and listen for the story it tells. Then look at a clock and summarize it, out loud, as a 60-second elevator pitch. Time's up! Next, boil it all down to one phrase that clearly states what you have to offer.

This is the promise embedded in your Career Narrative. Others might call it your Personal Brand. The brand is *what* you have to offer, and the narrative is *how* you sell it.

> **"The brand is what you have to offer, and the narrative is how you sell it."**

YOUR PERSONAL BRAND IS YOUR REPUTATION, AND YOUR REPUTATION IS YOUR BRAND

How does the world-at-large perceive you? What do people say about you when you're out of earshot? Do they say great things, or is your reputation in question?

It may seem contemporary; in truth individual branding was introduced by Napoleon Hill in 1937 when he wrote *Think and Grow Rich*. The subject has a lot more buzz and credibility today, and turns up in many forms, from the succession of celebrity-branded products and business ventures (think Sean Combs, Jennifer Lopez and Martha Stewart), through the endless stream of startups and internet ventures, on down to you and your webpage or blog.

When all is said and done, your branding works best through simple terms, with purposeful positioning, and from a unique point of view. How powerful to be in charge of every aspect, especially online! It's *your* brand, you own it. It doesn't belong to the government, a huge corporation, or some out-of-control social media site. It isn't regulated by licenses or permits. It is wide open to your own development, creative input, and control.

In the marketing world, how you present your unique point of view is called the unique selling point (aka USP). The term was developed by television advertising pioneer Rosser Reeves of Ted Bates & Company, and it was first used as a theory to highlight the underlying strategies in successful advertising campaigns of the 1940s. Your unique selling point could just as effectively be used to describe your personal brand in the job market and marketplace.

> *"Your unique selling point could just as effectively be used to describe your personal brand in the job market and marketplace."*

"Tell me about yourself" is the most common opener in job interviews. The subtext is really two blunt questions: "Why would I care about you?" and "What is your value?" The most effective answer is a brief statement of your personal brand, which you can easily prepare in the exercise before the mirror that I outlined above. State the promise at the heart of your Career Narrative, or USP, first, in one phrase. Next elaborate it in a 60 second elevator pitch. When your interviewer replies with follow up questions, you'll, of course, have responses from your resume, and also be able to share some compelling stories from exploring your work and career.

Now you have a foundation for: 1) what makes you unique, 2) what you have to offer, and 3) how to present it. It is now condensed and to the point. Next, let's reverse that reductive process and add more layers and depth in the streamlined and structured approach in the next section.

REWRITE YOUR CAREER NARRATIVE IN SIX EASY ACTIONS

These six steps are no-frills, to the point, and supported by the specificity of the questions.

1. *Set your goals.* Be specific and clearly define your objectives. Do you want to become known as the best manager in your niche? Do you want to land a job at a larger company? Are you looking to secure a promotion?
2. *Do lots of research.* What is your competition doing? How did your role models become successful? What advice does your mentor have for you?
3. *Set yourself apart.* What unique qualities do you bring to your niche in the market? What adjectives do you want people to use when they speak of you? What is the voice you want people to hear in your blog? What do you want your personal brand to convey?

4. *Acknowledge your level of success.* How do people currently perceive you? How large is the gap between your current achievements and where you want to be in three, five, or ten years? What do you want to change and what are your reasons?

5. *Set your strategy.* What action steps will you take to move you to the next level? How can you be sure they are practical and realistic? What is a reasonable timeline? How can you build accountability into the process? How will you evaluate your success?

6. *Manage your interconnectivity.* Proactively align all aspects of your story and brand, and keep them in sync. Ensure all your social media outlets use the same language. Does your LinkedIn profile use the same phrases and keywords as your resume? Do you have conflicting Tweets and Facebook posts floating around? Do you have a professional photo that represents the same image that you project when meeting face to face? Does the voice of your blogs echo your presentation in person?

CREATIVITY IS DRIVING YOUR CAREER NARRATIVE

In addition to being a career and executive coach, I am also a playwright. Like a lot of artists, I once held the notion that my creative work was a labor of love, and I faced a call for more practical endeavors to pay the bills. Founding a post-recession resume writing business five years ago was another such effort.

I soon realized that I was most effective in serving my clients when I dug deep to learn where they stopped in pursuit of their goals. In this regard, I was already coaching. Getting certification and rebranding myself as a career coach was inevitable, and I was doing precisely what I was coaching my clients to do – moving through to the next level.

In the process of refining my awareness of new clients, I found myself analyzing them as if they were characters in one of my scripts. They faced challenges, their story was told with a series of obstacles, and I was committed to finding innovative ways to fulfill their hopes and dreams. This all seemed less certain with fictional characters; the goals were clearer and more concretely defined with real clients. Yes, in real life it was just as easy, and in many ways easier, to see a beneficial, fulfilling conclusion – or happy ending. The client gets the job, or the promotion, and he or she is clearly at a new level of success.

> *"It is the best of both worlds, freedom to move between the categories of art and commerce."*

I realized that I had the same approach to both coaching and playwriting in a single moment I can only call an epiphany. Ever since, each new client is fascinating, and each of their stories is a gift to me. It is the best of both worlds, freedom to move between the categories of art and commerce. I am fully engaged in the flow of their narrative and completely invested in seeing it all unfold. To put it more simply, I am passionate about seeing what happens next.

THREE OF MY FAVORITE SUCCESS STORIES

Meet Chet. He was a developer in gaming. His core strength was digital concept development. When he first contacted me, he was unhappy with how his career was progressing at the large media company that employs him. He was hired for a part-time position, worked his way up to a full-time role involving design and production, and assumed increasing responsibility over the course of six years. While Chet was operating at an executive level and working closely with senior vice presidents, his reputation was still rooted in a wunderkind/geek sort of brand. He was underpaid, overworked, and not really taken as seriously as he deserved.

He wanted to quit and find a new job in a fresh start with more appreciation and better compensation. In the process of evaluating his strengths and achievements, it became clear that one of his chief talents, which he had honed and perfected over the years, was being a "kickass pitchman". He had developed many games and apps that held huge potential for amplifying the brand and increasing the exposure of certain animated television characters. Another layer of value was the potential back-end products and tie-ins. To make it all happen, he had to sell the executives on each project he had so passionately developed.

I pointed out to Chet that he was already selling them on his projects, so why not sell them on his career? He was a familiar figure in the organization, and clearly vital to the success of their department, and the larger company overall. We updated his resume, reworked and refined his Career Narrative, and rehearsed his presentation prior to his performance review. The result? He was given a promotion, an executive title, and the salary he deserved.

Meet Hal. He was doing very well in a new executive role, the result of years of dedicated work marketing in the technology industry. I had prepared his resume, which he has used to find two new jobs since our initial engagement. He contacted me to help refine his personal brand and interconnectivity, starting with LinkedIn. At the time, he simply had his employment history posted. It told a story that was not terribly compelling and didn't begin to express his passion and insights for his particular niche in the technology market.

On LinkedIn, his profile lacked personality, a unique selling point and, most importantly, his voice. I knew him, and furthermore, I knew his compelling, vital voice. The challenge was to channel that into a format as businesslike as LinkedIn. I asked him to share his vision for his career and listened carefully as I took notes. I then asked him to write down a free-flowing version of that same story in the same language he used when he was alone and working at his desk. We combined the two scripts, one in his everyday spoken voice, the other written in his work language, and synthesized the two by adding some insights and paraphrasing. Then we condensed it into a unified statement that was equal parts vision, career summary, and mission statement. He was astonished by how clearly and succinctly it nailed his personal brand in the first person, even though he didn't remember articulating most of it. Now that the voice is down pat, we're working on his webpage and blogs to establish his brand more firmly as a leader in his industry.

Meet Cameron. His career was indeed fascinating, only not from a predetermined career path. When we first started working together, we joked about the challenge of what to do with such a jack-of-all-trades. His occupations included fireman, a cowboy on a Texas ranch, a chef (mentored by a visionary in the food world), running a charitable outreach for hungry families, ski instructor, and teacher for EMS certification. He was managing a Bed & Breakfast at the time, and had been given the task of turning around a decline in business. His Career Narrative was full of amazing stories, colorful characters, and rich detail; and challenging to shoehorn into one role and sell it all in a unifying brand.

We detected a theme in his stories and key accomplishments: he knew how to turn around a troubled business, free of anyone's certification, and free of validation from an HR department. You can see the value in that sort of talent. We've since branded Cameron as a consultant for privately owned businesses, and an entirely new level of engagement, employment, and possibilities has opened up.

Your Career Narrative is Evolving

"I just don't buy it." Ever heard someone say that after hearing a story? Like it or not, your career must be bought too. The importance is everywhere, for every career, it's the way forward.

In his bestseller, *To Sell Is Human*, Daniel Pink proposes the provocative notion that we are all in sales now, and most everything we do is to move others, which is actually a kind of marketing. This promotion of an individual brand happens in a big way for some; for most of us, it's a more subtle, step-by-step process that's grounded in the details of our work in everyday life. This is an ongoing process that pushes at a ceiling as the same story, and yet your Career Narrative can always be retold – and powerfully so. Your success can leap to the next level through your ongoing story, and your rebranding can be sold and bought in a moving, compelling way.

> ***"Your success can leap to the next level through your ongoing story, and your rebranding can be sold and bought in a moving, compelling way."***

It's been said that nothing is perfect in this world. This doesn't mean you can't keep on perfecting your Narrative.

Brian Beatty is a student and teacher of compelling careers – how they grow, attain enduring success, and sustain their impact. He invested over six years of research and experience in the subject, and is now concentrating on executive and business coaching.

Driven by an unending curiosity for narrative, Brian naturally developed his coaching from crafting resumes. Each career has a history, each resume a unique story, and Brian feels honored listening to clients tell their stories. Coaching emerged from posing questions and listening to answers. How do you describe challenges? Where is the leverage in reaching the next level? How can you tell it – and sell it – more effectively?

Brian progressed through levels in coaching by engaging motivated professionals, creative executives, and talented entrepreneurs in a full spectrum of careers. He challenges consultants, innovators, and small business owners to explore niches, and re-imagine their brand, identity, and web presence.

Brian owns a culinary food walk business in Brooklyn called Eat Drink Brooklyn. He is also an avid author of stage plays and blogs. He loves the collaborations he continues to discover.

www.BrianBeattyCoaching.com

GETTING A GRIP ON TIME
by Charlie Kiss

As a coach, one of the more common requests I get has to do with time management. The one high truth about time to understand and accept is that time is finite. We may not have a clue as to how much time we have in total; the reality is there are always only 60 minutes in an hour, 24 hours in a day, 7 days in a week, and so on. We all love to throw phrases around like "when I find the time" or "when I can make some time" knowing that in realty, there is only so much time available. You will not find time laying around, and while you cannot technically make more time then you have, you can, and must, take time from other areas to invest in a different cause when appropriate.

> **"Time is in some ways like sleep**
> **- once you have lost it you cannot get it back."**

This fact is unlikely a surprise for anyone. We have all dealt with demands that have taken time from other areas. Often our mistakes are made when we try to catch up with the time that was lost or try to ignore where the stolen time came from instead of understanding, owning, and intentionally managing the time we have. Time is in some ways like sleep – once you have lost it you cannot get it back. Wasting energy to try and recover lost time just takes away from something else. Accept it and move on. Understand it and move on with confidence. In the next few pages I will be bringing out some observations and tools to use when coaching others on managing their time. Through making discoveries and owning our actions we develop the confidence to take control of our time. As coaches, we are examples of the practices we wish to support; while this is intended to be the coach's perspective, we can apply the ideas to our own benefit.

So what is the key to getting a grip on the time you have? In a word, control. If we do not take conscious control of the demands on our time, those placing the demands will attempt to take what they want without regard for our other demands. Most of us have heard statements like "the squeaky wheel gets the grease" or "put out the biggest fire first." Statements like that are knee jerk reactions to answering demands that are usually without thought or prioritization. While you may have a squeaky wheel that requires grease, you might also have a wobbly wheel about to fall off that is quiet. Understanding the demands, where they come from, and determining your own priorities empowers a person to manage their time more effectively. While you cannot make more time, effective use of your time will prevent you from wasting time. Coaching an individual on time management can be challenging; some people do not want to be honest with themselves, and others may not feel they have the right to control certain aspects of their time. We start by understanding how our time is spent. Once a person has a better understanding of the demands on their time, they can identify who is placing those demands and actively decide how to invest their time wisely.

BECOMING AWARE OF YOUR TIME

For many of us, time is one of the slipperiest commodities we have to deal with on a regular basis. To get a grip on the time we have, understand several things like how much time we have, who is using our time, and how best to manage our time. We can start by understanding how we use our time. We have expected demands on our time – time to eat, sleep, work – time for all the things required to maintain our health or support our lifestyle. There are at least four basic time groups and I am sure you can think of many sub groups that all fit nicely into these four.

1. *Family time*
This demand is different for many people: you may have children, large families, small families, near and far relatives, those by blood, marriage, or otherwise adopted, including pets.

2. *Work time*
Most of us have mortgages to pay, bills that come due, we have to eat. How a person defines work time is completely up to them; many define it as the time that they have to spend to earn a living or maintain a lifestyle. However you define it, you know what it is.

3. *Friend time*

Time we spend with those outside of our family with whom we share interests.

4. *Me time*

A personal favorite of mine, how much me time is ideal varies by personality type, some want very little and for others it is a requirement to recharge and replenish the tanks so we can be effective for the other time demands.

While there may be some unexpected components from time to time, the majority of these demands are known. Some people overwhelm themselves with the known demands in their lives and seek help for cutting an overwhelming list into bite-sized chunks. For others it is the unexpected demands that present the greatest challenges: the flat tire on the way to work or a sudden demand because of an unknown deadline. Life is full of unexpected demands that we want to find a way to address. As unexpected demands are realized they contribute to the list of known demands and can make the chore seem unbearable if they are not reasonably dispatched in a timely manner. Unexpected demands are usually driven by one crisis or another and may be referred to as crisis demands.

It is important that we mention both the importance of structuring time to accomplish both known and unexpected crisis demands, and to also look at balance. I mention four types of time as one example of a way to illustrate the point that we all do more than meet our demands, we also balance our own requirements. If we take all of our friend time away to meet work demands we will eventually find our friends have left us for others who have the time for them. Only the individual can define their balance and we are all different. While it may be acceptable to take time away from one area to meet a demand in another, be careful to identify and understand the impact of taking that time away. Controlling your time only begins with understanding how to use it better. Realizing where you can take time from and what the impact will be are keys to getting a productive and meaningful grip on time.

A primary lesson in getting a grip on time is identifying and removing the unknown and misunderstood as much as possible.

> *"Only the individual can define their balance and we are all different."*

We all have only so much time at our disposal and unless we control how it is allocated, somebody else will. Imagine if you had no idea how much money you had in the bank or who was taking some out? When you go to the store, how confident are you be that your debit card will work? The better you understand the demands on your time and who is making those demands, and the more you take control of the time you have, the better your time will be spent and the better you will know where you can take what you want when you want it. Instead of letting others control us, look at how we choose to spend our time. We will start by looking at known demands and later discuss crisis demands.

ARE YOU DROWNING IN A SEA OF THINGS THAT JUST HAVE TO GET DONE?

These are known or expected demands. When coaching the type of person who is overwhelmed by the apparent number of things to be done, simplify the pile. One method is a top ten list. An excellent homework exercise is to have the person write a list of what they feel must be done, or in other words the demands that are lingering and causing the feeling of not having enough time. In some cases that may be a challenge in itself. Make sure that things on the list are things that the person has direct influence over and can do without outside intervention. For example, if the demand is to make reservations for a business trip and the dates are not known, then the demand is not relevant. A concern yes, not a demand. While it might be replaced with looking up the dates for travel it might also be waiting on action from somebody outside our control and therefore a future demand that is pending. Some may write page after page anticipating demands well into the future or be excessively granular. It may be important to define boundaries like only high level demands or set a time limit for writing down all known demands and stopping no matter what in 20 minutes. In reviewing the homework, review the list with the coachee and reach agreement to identify and strike anything not actually a current or realistic demand. Be careful not to judge or project your own impressions. This list is about their lives and they have to come to the conclusions on their own what is relevant or not. Look for opportunities to ask powerful questions. For example, one powerful question might be "How can we eliminate or decrease the possibility or intensity of this demand recurring?" The next step is to pick ten and only ten to set actions on. One way is to prioritize the overall list, if that is just too difficult simply take the first ten valid known demands on the list. Those with highest priority are usually the first ones you think about (unless they depend on something further down the list in which case they are not current demands until the prerequisites are completed).

Now make an action list for only the top ten current demands. Remember to make SMART actions. A Specific action which is Measurable, Achievable, Relevant, and most importantly, Time bound. When one demand is completed replace it with another from the list sticking to SMART rules. The limit of ten keeps it manageable. The key is understanding and control. Understanding what realistic and valid demands are and limiting the focus to a manageable number keeps the challenge under control. Before you know it, the list will be depleted and you can put away this tool until the next time you want it.

The list can be a powerful tool for helping clients maintain control over their time. A fellow coach recently shared this example with me. "One of my clients feels compelled to be responsive to her family, even to a fault. While she attempts to plan her days, she often finds she will rearrange everything at a moment's notice to accommodate a request from a family member. Having this list handy gives her the power to refer to a tangible list and ask, "What has to come off my list to accommodate this request?" "Is it worth it? Is accommodating this new request more beneficial than accomplishing what I had already planned for today?" If the answer is yes, she makes the adjustment. If the answer is no, she finds a way to decline or postpone the request."

> *"What has to come off my list to accommodate this request?"*

DOES A BARRAGE OF CRISIS DEMANDS OVERWHELM YOU ON A REGULAR BASIS?

What if the problem is unexpected demands? We are very lucky that there are many types of tools to help us capture information so we can review and analyze our unexpected demands and the reactions to those demands. One such tool is the ages old log book; one challenge may be determining how to incorporate it into our daily lives. We can use actual pen and paper, computers, smart phones, or any number of devices to collect our data, and thanks to technology we also have the cloud so we can access our log from multiple devices if that is something with which the coachee is comfortable. They record the unexpected demands on their time and the urgency. It is imperative that urgency is well defined; I have had success with a simple scale of 1 to 4.

1 = Time critical, has to be done immediately.
2 = Urgent, must be done today.
3 = Required, could be accomplished in the next few days.
4 = Nice to have done.

Write the priorities down somewhere so they will be understood and consistent. Consistency is important. A point to emphasize is that the level of urgency they provide be their feeling of the urgency in the moment; encourage the individual not to analyze the unexpected demand too deeply. It is all about feelings at this point of the journey. It is also important to stress that this is not a to-do list. We can incorporate information from this demand log to help us with a to-do or action list later.

If they are challenged by logging how their time is being demanded, there may be several things getting in the way. Sometimes the unexpected demands come so rapidly that there is no time to record the demands. After all, we are asking them to use a resource they already feel they do not have enough of, time. One alternative is to define log points. While I have found it most helpful when the log is updated at least 3 times a day, there are those who have been successful updating only at mid-day and evening. At the agreed on times, have the coachee backfill the list to show unexpected demands and to rate the urgency perceived at the time. It is not important if they miss a few. If the demand felt like a 1 when it hit you, while in reflection when you write it down you perceive it as a 3, then the urgency is a 1. The important takeaway is the feeling and demand as it was perceived in the moment. This cannot be overstated.

Commitment to a demand log is seven days a week, no exceptions. Avoid the log being too detailed or granular. Getting ready for work or taking out the trash are irrelevant, expected routine maintenance type demands, it is the demands outside of those to identify and understand. Additionally, have the coachee ask this question at the end of the day, "How do you feel you managed your time today?" Give it a rating of 1 to 10 where 10 indicates that you managed your time well and 1 indicates complete chaos. This can empower you to look back and identify patterns which can help you identify what other factors impact time.

Roadblocks can be the tools themselves. Be careful not to overly influence others with your methods; it is OK to share options. The coachee must use what works well for them. If time logging is not successful at first, ask what is getting in the way, what can make it easier, what do they want? Different tools are appropriate for different situations. Quick notes on the fly with a smart phone app or voice recording consolidated into a log at logging points instead of trying to use the same tool throughout the day is an option. Ask questions or role-play a moment where they felt it hard to keep track of things. Explore using different tools to help identify what works best for them. Time itself can be the challenge so make sure that it is known upfront that in order to get the time in the long term it starts with understanding the demands on time so it may require taking time from other things. It could be as simple as consciously going to bed 15 minutes later for a few weeks, or taking 45 minutes for lunch instead of an hour. Sometimes we are supported by identifying the time to log our time demands as demands themselves. Getting someone in the practice of consciously taking time from one activity to perform another is, after all, the whole point of this exercise. Celebrate early discoveries, and maintain the effort. Early realizations and progress are great; the long-term goal is to become the master of your time and that usually requires a longer effort past winning the first few battles.

WHO IS REALLY IN CHARGE OF YOUR TIME?

Crisis demands are typically made by others. The next question after you have started the habit of keeping a demand log may be to identify who is really in control of your time.
This is an optional and sometimes important addition to the process. It makes sense that others are making demands on

your time. The key is that you are aware of it and realize that regardless of the source of the demand, you are the one who is really in control of your time. Parents do it all the time with their children. Children make many demands on their parent's time, demands like feed me and wash me cannot be ignored; the question of when is what we control. Some people may want to add an additional column to their demand log to identify who is making the demand. Recognize that some people may identify all demands as their own when they actually come from others. Because it had to be done is an unacceptable response for who makes the demand. Dig past the symptom to the cause or root of the unexpected demand. Another person's perception of need and urgency may be misunderstood or misinterpreted. Look at the demand log example below.

Unexpected Demand	Priority	By?
Compile report of expenses for the last three months	1	Boss
Pick up Johnny early from school (sick)	1	Johnny/School
Rewrite the shipping procedures to include new corporate policy	2	Boss

Keep in mind that we are looking at demands for understanding and awareness. Compiling the report was perceived as an immediate demand. Did you ask when it had to be done? Is your assumption based on perception or facts? Picking Johnny up from school because he is sick is a negotiable demand. Can someone else pick him up? Will it matter if you take an additional five or ten minutes to finish or accomplish something else first? The priority for the demand is valid; how it is met is debatable. Rewriting procedures urgent? Must be done today? What gave the perception of urgency? Was it challenged?

Identifying where the demand is coming from may illuminate a trend or source that can be investigated further. If a single person is a source of a majority of critical and urgent demands then the coachee can dig deeper and explore that relationship. Are the perceptions realistic? How negotiable is the demand? Is the heightened demand an indication of another issue to be discussed and explored? Getting a grip on our time can also mean getting a grip on our relationships. Challenges in managing time are sometimes a symptom of other challenges.
Keeping a log of our demands and understanding where our time is spent, and who is demanding it, are excellent methods to identify areas for further attention.

> *"Getting a grip on our time can also mean getting a grip on our relationships."*

As a coach it is advantageous to review demand logs periodically. People typically have many demands on their time with varying frequency. There may be periods of high demand that cascade into multiple days at some regular interval. Life is full of repeating patterns, some are obvious like the holidays every year, summer vacations, and school schedules to name a few. Many of us prepare for the most well-known cycles in various ways, saving money for the holidays or planning vacations in advance, because we are aware of the demands in advance so we make a reasonable effort to be ready for them when the time comes. Reviewing a demand log over weeks or even months can illuminate cycles and once we are aware of the cyclical demands we can prepare.

> *"Reviewing a demand log over weeks or even months can illuminate cycles and once we are aware of the cyclical demands we can prepare."*

How often a coach reviews a demand log is a judgment call. A good start is at two weeks to see what is starting to reveal itself. The coachee is the one who must analyze their logs and look for trends and epiphanies. It is the coach's responsibility to guide them without interpreting, directing, or judging. How to look at the information is sometimes a challenge as well because the sheer scale of information can be overwhelming. This is the reason a well-defined structure is appropriate while gathering the information. The coachee should look at complete individual days and compare them to other complete days. A tool like a spreadsheet program works well for some people where each new day is a new tab in their workbook. Others have had success with calendar tools capturing demands rather than schedules, and there is the old stand-by paper log book. Sometimes the first discovery is that the initial tool is not working as well as was expected. If that is the case then revisit what tools are available and make a change. Changing tools and starting over is a success so treat it as such.

TAKE CONTROL OF YOUR OWN TIME!

As we identify issues we immediately start exploring ways to improve. One of the simplest, and at the same time most difficult, is empowering a person to identify where and when to say no. Equally important is how to say no. The challenge is saying no in a way that is respectful or saying yes in a way that is mutually agreeable. When a child asks for a new skateboard it is acceptable to just say no. What about when your boss asks you to work on a Saturday when you already had plans? One of the primary reasons for poor judgment in time management is an error in perception, usually due to a lack of understanding the actual demand. Ask questions! "What must be completed by Saturday and what can wait until next week?" Offer alternatives. "Can I put in extra time this week to accomplish it?" Barter for your time. "Saturday is difficult for me, can I get this to you by Tuesday?" You can avoid the use of the word no by being creative with options and alternatives. This is another great opportunity for role-play to train the coachee how to think on their feet and respond creatively and powerfully.

ADDITIONAL TOOLS FOR GETTING A GRIP ON TIME ARE SHELVING AND TIME MAPPING

Shelving is the permission to stop working on one action or task to take care of a higher priority demand. We all do this on a regular basis; many are unaware of how to do it properly. Shelving is a good tool when it adheres to the same SMART rules we use for action steps and goal setting. More specifically the time-bound part. When we have to shelve a task it must have a shelf life. For example, if I usually mow the lawn on Sunday and it happens to be Mother's Day, I can shelve the lawn until later as long as it is time bound. I will mow the lawn Tuesday night instead of going bowling. Can a shelved task be re-shelved? Absolutely, as long as the task is still time bound. Only the responsible person can decide their priorities and be responsible for their decisions.

Time Mapping is helpful to some who want more structure to maintain their demands. Time mapping is like scheduling only instead of scheduling actual tasks it is scheduling windows of availability. For instance some people map Saturday morning for golf and Saturday afternoon for chores. Some map date nights where only the intent is scheduled; the specifics are decided by other means. The takeaway here is that time mapping brackets time where certain things are expected to occur representing an opportunity. Remember that ultimately everyone controls their own time.

LAST WORDS

> *"...there are no credit cards for time."*

Time is finite; there is only so much of it. Like money, some of it has to go to commitments including mortgage, food, and clothes. Or in the case of time, to work, family, friends. If we have money left over it is called discretionary funds that we can spend as we see fit, like on gifts or movie tickets. Discretionary time is a wonderful thing when we have it and sought after when we do not, and unfortunately there are no credit cards for time. If we do not have discretionary funds available we decide where we will reduce our expenses if we want to spend money on something else. The same is true for time. If you want to spend time in one place, you decide where you can take time from. Deciding to go back to school for a graduate degree? Lock up your golf clubs, tell your friends you will miss them, promise your loved one an awesome vacation when you get back, and remember to schedule a big party at the end to let them know you are back. Balance is important and it is imperative that as coaches we ask about what is important to help our coachee achieve the balance they desire. Support getting a grip on time and encourage control and balance. How much analysis is enough analysis? As with most things in coaching, it is up to the coachee. While I have seen the rare person get all they can out of these methods in three to four weeks, many carry it out 12 weeks and more. As long as there are new discoveries and progress being made there is reason to continue. In this method, discovery and adjustments are accomplished in parallel; challenges are worked on simultaneously with new discoveries. When the process slows or stops making forward progress, it is obviously time to stop. At least for now.

Charlie Kiss is a Certified Master Coach with a Bachelor of Science in Management from the University of Phoenix and a Master of Business Administration from Texas A&M. He has been in management, coaching, and teaching for over 30 years. Charlie's specialties include Leadership, Communication, Time Management, and Staff Development. Charlie started in the United States Navy's Leadership and Management Skills training program. He recognizes the value of coaching and the impact of helping others realize and transform themselves to fulfill their vision. The Kiss method is unlock Knowledge you possess, Instruction to leverage that knowledge, Strategy to implement, and Success naturally follows.

Charlie has built a reputation as a valued resource to help others overcome their challenges and to help those at varying levels of management improve their skills to make them more effective leaders, communicators and resource developers. As an Executive Coach, Charlie enjoys building new relationships, learning about challenges, and developing unique methods to help people identify and overcome their barriers to success.

Charlie is a member of the International Coach Federation and Houston Coaches certified by Center for Coaching Certification.

www.coachkiss.com

Conscious Leadership:
Its Impact on Personal and Organizational Change
by Jennifer A. Connell

Leaders today face a complex environment rife with financial uncertainty and extremely low levels of employee engagement. Change comes at a dizzying speed, from changes in social norms of how we communicate with each other to technological advancement to changes in employee and stakeholder expectations—all played out amid an economic uncertainty that spans the globe.

In order to deal effectively with the current challenges we face, everyone employed in organizations will benefit from thinking in new ways. Leaders in corporations, governments, non-governments organizations, armed forces, charities, not-for-profit corporations, partnerships, and education all must find more effective ways to engage their followers to adapt to and solve the challenges ahead. Organizations of all kinds are facing a crisis in employee engagement and must improve their ability to adapt to organizational change. Leaders cannot do the job alone; involving everyone throughout the organization from the executive leaders to the front line employees will cultivate sustainable success.

One example includes America's schools that suffer great consequences due to lack of engagement. While not judged on the basis of quarterly financial performance, schools are regularly held accountable for student achievement on standardized tests. Schools with low test scores face reductions in financial support, as well as public scrutiny of administration and staff.

> *"Conscious Leadership is defined as the practice of self-awareness, honoring and respecting the interconnections and interdependencies with those in the organization, and eliciting the potential of others."*

Holistic approaches to leadership create opportunities for leaders to embrace and practice humanistic values, such as treating others with dignity and respect, empowering others, and exhibiting compassion and empathy. These characteristics, when taken together can be termed conscious leadership. When leaders attend to their internal landscape by cultivating self-awareness, and lead from that place, they honor the interdependent connections in the organization. This approach may be much more effective than traditional leadership styles in eliciting the potential of others.

For purposes of my work as a leadership coach, Conscious Leadership is defined as the practice of self-awareness, honoring and respecting the interconnections and interdependencies with those in the organization, and eliciting the potential of others.

When we reframe leadership as a duty to honor, serve, and guide others, acknowledging that our actions, behaviors, and decisions affect everyone in the organization, people reconnect with what is meaningful and lead from that place of awareness.

I was part of a team that worked with two such leaders a few years ago. After the initial client intake, we developed an agenda to foster individual and organizational effectiveness, increase accountability, and enhance engagement. The cornerstone of our engagement was introducing the leaders to a technique that cultivated effective conversations. We also coached them extensively on how on to use the technique, and, in turn, the coaching cascaded through the leadership levels. This ultimately fostered sustainable resolutions to their prioritized desired outcomes.

> *"If you want one year of prosperity, grow grain.*
> *If you want ten years of prosperity, grow trees.*
> *If you want 100 years of prosperity, grow people."*
> ***Chinese Proverb***

What follows is an illustration of how this client, a school district, transitioned from dysfunctional to achieving its desired organizational change outcomes through the application of Conscious Leadership consulting and coaching.

MEET ONE OF AMERICA'S SCHOOL DISTRICTS

To put things in perspective, the background of the school district is presented first, followed by the Conscious Leadership consulting-coaching process and then the findings that suggest Conscious Leadership elicited sustainable organizational change, marked by effective conversations, increased commitment and accountability, and enhanced engagement.

The Department of Education showed the student population for the school district used in this study was 2,665 in 2008 and on average the student to teacher ratio was 14 to 1 spread throughout three elementary schools, the middle school, and the high school.

Though this case study reflects the consulting-coaching process in a school district, it is easy to see how similar dysfunctional issues can infect organizations of any size. As you read their compelling success story, I invite you to consider their issues and relate them to experiences you have likely had at one time or another in your personal or professional life.

INTRODUCING CONSCIOUS LEADERSHIP

Starting in the 2006-2007 academic year, the school district shifted its executive level leadership when it hired a new superintendent and assistant superintendent. The superintendent stepped into her new position with a strong passion to create change. When asked what her vision was she said, "I want to increase student achievement, increase the level of teaching and learning in the district and have people be happy about it, and about coming to work." Despite fractured workplace relationships, lack of vision, and weak student achievement when they came into their positions, these leaders believed that they could make a difference in the student's success and in the community at large. Aware of the school district's history of strained relationships, the incoming executive leaders, superintendent, and assistant superintendent made relationships their top priority. This was punctuated when the assistant superintendent said, "What I noticed right away is that until I could get people to work through all of the things that we needed to be able to work through, I had to first build relationships. We really needed to work on relationships within the staff and administrators and students and parents and board members."

> *"...there is a reinforcing loop ..."*

The Conscious Leadership approach used with this school district included introducing them to the concept of effective conversations and coaching the leaders on how to conduct them. Indeed it was the cornerstone to the change initiative because based on experience and observation there is a reinforcing loop of influence between the quality of conversation, the quality of relationships, and the quality of the results achieved.

Effective conversations utilize conversation guidelines. Adapted from the dialogic principles as discussed in *Dialogue and the Art of Thinking Together* (Isaacs, 1999), these guidelines are akin to listening between the words of the speaker, speaking candidly from a place of authenticity, reserving personal judgments, honoring and respecting difference in perspectives, and slowing the conversation. Dialogue enhances a team's capacity to think collectively and symbiotically. Anecdotal evidence suggests that as team members practiced dialogue in this manner, they grew individually and collectively, which enhanced the organization's capacity to learn. This, in turn, increased effectiveness.

> *"Dialogue enhances a team's capacity to think collectively and symbiotically."*

At the beginning of a coaching relationship, clients identify the top priorities they want to improve or change. The process then begins to draw sharp focus on achieving their desired outcomes by developing and implementing strategic action plans. The first and significant priority we addressed was the workplace climate, which according to many administrators, was dismal and unproductive. The instructional program specialist, who had been in the district for 13 years and was in the classroom before becoming an administrator, shared that the relationships between the administrators and the teacher's association were historically strained. She said, "We were stuck in the dynamics of 30 years of animosity and hatefulness." The teachers felt as if some of the administrators were out to get them and that when teachers voiced their concerns, the administrators would hold the information against them. This contention was also physically visible in the workplace as the assistant superintendent observed: "Three years ago, no one talked to each other. People had big posters and stickers all over their windows and on their doors so nobody could see in and nobody could see out. Anytime anybody asked anybody to do something, they would send them a letter telling them they had crossed the line, and there were several grievances filed. There was so much fear here."

APPLICATION OF CONSCIOUS LEADERSHIP: EMBRACED AND INTEGRATED

Coaching combined with implementation of the Conscious Leadership approach and a focus on building relationships and increasing student achievement surfaced a new energy in the system. They also gained momentum and experienced sustainable changes including the following:

1. The Conscious Leadership approach created a conversational space for change.

2. Conversation fueled organizational change through commitment.

3. Increased teamwork, accountability, engagement, and a vivid vision of their desired future state.

1. The Conscious Leadership Approach Creates a Conversational Space for Change

This leadership approach was adopted and practiced at first by the superintendent and assistant superintendent. We coached the superintendent and assistant superintendent and found their commitment to effective conversations fostered internal support, listening, and trust—all of which had a positive impact on employees.

As great leaders do, the superintendent also exhibited continuous support for her executive leaders by consistently modeling and encouraging use of the conversation guidelines. The assistant superintendent explained in a tone of sincere appreciation the superintendent's dedication to the practice of listening for understanding, one of the conversation guidelines: "She would listen for so long that sometimes I would think, 'I think she's tuning me out.' Then later on, what I shared would come up in conversation. She heard it all and was thinking about what I said. She listens and then uses the information later on to acknowledge people."

Demonstrating her ability to listen for understanding, the superintendent practiced the conversation guidelines by using statements such as: "Let me see if I understand you" or "If I hear you correctly, you are saying ..." and then would repeat back to people in her own words what she thought they meant. Interestingly, one of her direct reports stated, "Even if she does not agree with what I say, she makes the time to really hear it, and that is huge to me. I feel extraordinarily valued!"

The superintendent's commitment paid off in beneficial ways. The perceptions of feeling valued and being heard were seemingly perpetuated through continuous support and coaching from the top-level leaders. Their employment of the conversation guidelines generated trust. Employees were quick to point out the link between trust and behavior, as the human resource specialist shared about the superintendent: "She has confidence in the people that work for her. She trusts everyone is doing the job they were hired to do." The coaching process cascaded through the leadership team and transformed the intrapersonal relationships.

> *"The coaching process cascaded through the leadership team and transformed the intrapersonal relationships."*

The leaders' willingness to be coached cultivated a change in key relationships within the school district. The instructional program specialist said, "Prior to our current assistant superintendent, we did not get support and direction from central office." That support is vital. How was that support demonstrated? The high school principal responded, "This might sound simplistic, but as far as the assistant superintendent supporting my leadership development, most of the time it was just through conversations." Following the conversation guidelines they had learned through the consulting-coaching process opened the door to building rapport. They also increased trust in some as noted by the middle school principal who said, "The assistant superintendent willingly helped me out. I have never felt comfortable sharing things with other bosses."

2. Conversation Fueled Organizational Change Through Commitment

Of course, organizational changes do not happen overnight. They take conscious action, commitment and modeling to cultivate sustainability. We coached them on another one of their priorities, which was to develop the capacity to have structured conversations that produced committed outcomes. Historically, the information shared throughout the district was simply drifting into a void with no one taking committed actions.

Awareness and intention were integral to effective conversations, and with commitment and modeling, structured conversations using the conversation guidelines became accepted as an operating principle. The protocol was practiced during meetings, formal and informal, large and small. The meeting framework was not just about passing information along as the human resource specialist noted: "The whole idea of conversations is a crucial key. Conversation made us look at each other as individuals. We can all put out a piece of paper and share data, but we actually felt confident in the group that we were working with because we were having meaningful conversations." In this case, the superintendent and assistant superintendent's commitment to successful implementation of the practice was noticed as indicated by the elementary school principal: "The assistant superintendent always says, 'let's have a conversation.' I found myself adopting the same with my direct reports in our grade level meetings."

The superintendent and assistant superintendent believed structured conversation using the guidelines was critical to this organization's change initiative. The assistant superintendent's comment emphasized the role of awareness and intention and their impact on others: "I believe in the conversation at the moment. That is all you have is that conversation right then. Whatever you say, however you show up for somebody will either leave them inspired, enrolled, or motivated, or you can leave them in the space they were in or even do some damage."

3. Coaching Them to Work Together Increased Accountability and Enhanced Engagement

The coaching process also addressed another priority the leaders wanted to resolve—the lack of infrastructure, which perpetuated a level of ambiguity and permeated the organization. There were no priorities in place. The director of special education shared that the district was out of compliance with complex state regulations. This required that teachers be educated on the proper paperwork protocol to bring them into compliance. Faculty meetings were viewed both as complaint sessions and a waste of energy. The human resources specialist said, "We would get together as a group and just feed data that was affecting only our department to each other, and we all felt that it wasn't effective."

A notable result of the coaching process was the formation of accountability partners to ensure each individual produced the results to which they committed. In this organization, implementing Conscious Leadership and structured conversations encouraged them to work together and ultimately increased their level of accountability and engagement. Together they built an infrastructure for the organization. The superintendent's encouragement was supportive of the assistant superintendent's intention to build an infrastructure that fostered inclusiveness and encouraged people to work together to support student achievement. The coaching process elicited her behavior, which aligned to her purpose and values.

The above-mentioned actions resulted in the formation of a needs-assessment committee, about which the assistant superintendent said, "It was really the conversations we had together that helped people to become enrolled and motivated." She shared that these conversations were inclusive and illuminated their current reality and elicited information about what they collectively felt needed to be done. She said, "After collecting the data, we put together a list of district priorities and the staff embraced it. They even thanked the assessment committee for the work they did."

From a coaching perspective, true learning occurs when individuals metabolize and integrate new information to foster a change in behavior. To this point, it was important for the administrative leaders to examine and shift their negative and/or limiting beliefs to those that matched what the superintendent and assistant superintendent envisioned for the school district to set a solid foundation for change. The conversation guidelines were a means through which the assistant superintendent could empower them to create new realities for themselves. We emphasized the importance of and coached them how to identify their own and others' personal mental models. The technique cultivated deeper inquiry and enhanced opportunities to learn from one another. In doing so, team members were better able to learn from diverse thinking.

> *"Coaching offers a powerful process for fostering synergy, creativity, intuition, and teamwork."*

Teamwork—Coaching offers a powerful process for fostering synergy, creativity, intuition, and teamwork. Over time, teamwork was embraced and impacted this organization's change initiative. The superintendent was very clear about her intention: "The culture was changed so that everyone felt included. We believed that everyone in this district from the transportation coordinator to the food service director to the business manager contributed to the success of the students. Previously, they didn't see how they fit into the whole system of contributing to the student's success."

Teamwork became common at the administrator level within the school district as noted by the high school assistant principal who said, "We all worked together towards a common goal of having a topnotch school district so people want to send their children here because we are best in the county." The synergy and creativity began to flow and teamwork was seen at the staff level, too, as suggested by the high school principal who asserted, "Some departments that had the reputation of being reactionary, began collaborating, working together and showed great improvement."

Increased Accountability—As previously highlighted, the executive leaders were student-centered and encouraged every staff member in the district to contribute to the students' success. According to the high school principal, meetings were once considered information dumps and regurgitation sessions. We coached them to make accountability an expectation. We introduced them to a meeting protocol whereby their meetings started by first stating their purpose, followed by developing a shared understanding, and having an expectation that, at the end of a meeting attendees would take responsibility for seeing certain agenda items through to completion. They worked together to embrace this protocol and began conducting meetings that elicited committed actions from individuals. The new priorities combined with passion for student success, and accountability was an awkward transition for some at first. The executive leaders offered coaching support and the high school principal said, "If there were any issues, if things came up, we just talked our way through the different situations using the conversation guidelines. Therefore, there was flexibility, but also accountability; assistance was always available."

> *"Coaching is a powerful way to empower employees to set their own direction."*

Coaching is a powerful way to empower employees to set their own direction. One positive outcome achieved through the process is that the level of increased accountability cascaded down to the administrative leadership team. The elementary school principal acknowledged that being held accountable was new to her. She shared that when she goes to a professional conference, she is expected to inform the assistant superintendent about how she will put the new information to use with her staff to help them perform at a higher level. Her expectations, in turn, have changed: "I am holding my people more accountable than I did in the past." Now she coaches her staff about using new tools and information, and she follows up with them to find out what they have learned.

The accountability factor is of real value in one's personal or professional life —having others check up on one other to ensure they are meeting their agreed upon expectations is an effective part of the coaching process. Examples of increased accountability seen in this organization include those whose behavior suggested they were willing to work together and hold themselves accountable. The director of special education began asking herself, "What can I do to help people achieve, to have those conversations so in the long run what we do to help students is better?" The middle school principal asserted: "I completely embraced everyone. I realized that we all depended on each other. I started resolving conflicts using the conversation guidelines and while it took time, I saw the experience as positive. I included others, and I saw the organization becoming healthier because of this technique."

> *"Never doubt that a small group of thoughtful, committed citizens can change the world. Indeed, it is the only thing that ever has."* **Margaret Mead**

The coaching process fostered collaboration as it cascaded throughout the school district, and accountability became a shared effort throughout the organization. The instructional program specialist reported a higher level of accountability at the organizational level than existed in the past: "If we created assessments, there was no way to know if they were reliable, no way to measure results, because they were not field tested." She went on to highlight that any enrichment or remediation program adopted now is research based, and pre- and post-testing is conducted to ensure its efficacy. The school district now uses student data to drive decisions about how to best serve the students. One measure taken to hold the organization accountable to students is a regularly scheduled meeting every three weeks, designed to assess student achievement to ensure students were meeting required skill sets. As the superintendent explained, "Responsibility fell on us as teachers and administrators to figure out what we were going to do differently if a student wasn't learning, and how we would meet the individual student's need." Their commitment led to impressive results. The high school principal suggested that being accountable contributed to their goal of supporting student achievement: "The one thing I can point to is there was a focus on eliminating student failures that year. We set up an academic at risk team. Essentially, we coached the whole faculty on learning a new system, generating new forms, new deadlines, and new benchmarks. We constantly reinforced the importance of it. In the first quarter we reduced our failure rate by 43%."

"Their commitment led to impressive results."

A committed focus on working together increased the level of accountability throughout the system, and the findings suggest that the individual's engagement level was enhanced.

Enhanced Engagement—The executive leaders' passion about the student's success became contagious. It was important for employees to be coached to increase their professional engagement; the process built trust and fostered loyalty. The student attendance officer noted: "It started at the top with the superintendent and assistant superintendent." Their commitment to using conversation guidelines permeated the system and engendered a change among direct reports, as noted by the superintendent: "They changed their style of conversation and it cut down on the number of calls that I received from people who were upset." The assistant superintendent made it a priority to share her belief in the power of conversation and coached her team on a daily basis: "I worked on having conversations with people about reality and the way situations occurred for them. I helped them to understand that the way situations occurred for them is explained through the language they used, not just the words or verbiage, but also with their body language and with the way it felt when we walked into their office or a particular building. I helped them to understand they had the power to create their own futures."

The elementary school principal acknowledged that through coaching, her practice of listening for understanding enhanced her engagement: "I learned about and practiced asking more questions. I was listening and wanted more information from them, and people perceived it in the right way. Instead of me shooting info at them, we talked through it and our collective understanding increased. Their level of engagement increased; they had more buy-in."

Vivid Description of Their Future—The coaching process empowers individuals and groups to clarify their vision and desired future outcomes. In this organization, consulting and coaching addressed fundamental and critical infrastructure issues first. Then through additional focused coaching at their executive leadership retreat notable change happened on the team level as demonstrated by the leadership team's willingness to be educated and coached on how to create a shared vision and develop vivid descriptions of their future. The superintendent shared that after their retreat they realized how important it was to become informed of what was going on in all the organization's departments or each area of responsibility that related to the vivid description of the future they developed: "Unlike some other organizations where the vision is plastered in the front lobby and on the website but not paid much attention in their daily business activities, these executive leaders were committed to this vision becoming integrated within themselves personally and the system." Developing a shared understanding of the vision amongst the administrative leaders helped them derive personal meaning from it. From the assistant superintendent's perspective, they became stewards of the vision and it became integrated throughout the system. She said, "The organization's identity included all of us, separately and together. Having them create it and become enrolled in making sure it happened enabled them to, in turn, coach others to become aligned and engaged."

The vivid descriptions and focused commitment created synergy in the system as reflected in the director of special education who said she saw results with her personal goal which affected her direct reports: "Their level of achievement as professionals increased and that was part of my goal – to make them better with their students – all students – not just special education students."

The Conscious Leadership approach introduced via a combination of consulting and coaching reaped huge accomplishments as highlighted by the superintendent: "We just got a couple of letters acknowledging that for the growth we made in just the past three years in both math and reading is in the top 5%. The first letter we got said the nation. The second letter said in the state. That's something we celebrated with the teachers!"

In Conclusion – The Conscious Leadership approach indeed met the superintendent's expectations of wanting to increase student achievement, the level of teaching and learning in the district and have people be happy about it. The consulting-coaching process had a positive impact on communication, teamwork, accountability, and engagement, and fostered sustainable success in this organization. Change does not happen overnight, yet, the coaching process is incredibly valuable to making changes stick when used with discipline.

> *"The consulting-coaching process had a positive impact on communication, teamwork, accountability, and engagement, and fostered sustainable success in this organization."*

Research suggests there is a widespread concern that it is difficult to get people to integrate and use newly gained knowledge, thus ultimately resulting in a decline in personal fulfillment, loss in productivity and potentially decreased bottom line profitability. The Personnel Management Association highlights knowledge transfer as follows:

- Training Alone: 22%
- Training plus Coaching: 88%

Indeed it begs the question of whether it is time for you to consider Conscious Leadership and/or hiring a success strategy catalyst to explore creating fulfillment, effective results, and sustainable success in your personal and professional life!

Jennifer Connell, Success Strategy Catalyst, thrives when coaching and supporting individuals develop their internal capacity to lead, adapt to change, and achieve. She has a Master's in Organizational Systems, is a Certified Professional Coach, and a Certified Professional Behavior Analyst. She integrates multi-disciplinary professional and personal experience with integrity, humor, creativity, and passion.

Jennifer has assisted public, private, and non-profit clients including State Farm, Florida Department of Environmental Protection, City of West Palm Beach, school districts, The SELF Movement, Character Counts!, JEA, Blood Alliance, and Ricoh-USA. She has a unique ability for identifying the root cause then increasing capacities. An accomplished businesswoman with domestic and international experience, she has incorporated leading edge disciplines and tools to cultivate healthy communication and foster sustainable success.

After building and selling a business in New Jersey, Jennifer moved to Florida with her husband where she enjoys the beach, family time, community service, and working with individuals who welcome growth and change.

www.JenniferConnell.com

Coaching Others to Succeed in a VUCA World

by Maria Van Parys

In *The World Is Flat*, Thomas Friedman talks about the high-tech companies that failed to keep up with change and as a result failed. We have seen numerous technology firms succumb to the forces of change, for example: Atari, Netscape, Polaroid and Palm. In the wake of new technological and marketing advancements, these once successful, even pioneering companies, failed to sustain themselves over time.

This phenomenon is not exclusive to the high tech sector. In almost every industry, the ability to navigate these forces of change is what separates those that sustain success from those that struggle or worse yet, fail.

"Volatility, Uncertainty, Complexity, and Ambiguity"

These forces of change, whether driven by technology, globalization, demographics, consumer patterns, competition, economics, politics, or the environment, are what business leaders are now referring to as a "VUCA" environment. The acronym VUCA was first coined in the late 1990's by the military. Volatility, Uncertainty, Complexity, and Ambiguity are terms well understood by armed forces that stand ready in the face of the unknown. The term VUCA has grown significance beyond the military and rapidly changing business world to perhaps every facet of our life and world. In the Zulu language, the expression of VUCA means "to wake up". Perhaps this is a call to action. How do we navigate through and lead successful, productive lives amidst this chaotic and intimidating environment? In this chapter, we will take a deeper look at the new VUCA environment and explore how, as coaches, we can develop ourselves and others to manage effectively through the circumstances of our time.

The "V" in the VUCA stands for volatility. Volatility is like turbulence – instability with rapid change. In our world today, volatility is occurring with greater and greater frequency. A study by the Boston Consulting Group (BCG) found that half of the most turbulent financial quarters in modern times have occurred in the past ten years.

The "U" in the VUCA acronym stands for uncertainty. These uncertain times make it difficult for leaders to use past issues and events as predictors of future outcomes. The absence of predictability makes forecasting results almost impossible and even the simplest decision-making more challenging.

The "C" in VUCA stands for complexity. Rapidly changing technology, globalization, demographics, consumer patterns, competition, economic, political, and environmental shifts are a multiplex of forces that surround an organization and confound business decision-making.

The "A" in VUCA stands for ambiguity or lack of clarity. Ambiguous situations can be misleading and lend themselves to false or incomplete information. In business, operating without clarity can be reckless and lead to poor decision-making or paralyze progress simply out of fear of making any decision.

As a human resources professional, I work with other leaders and their teams and departments on implementing processes to help improve individual and organizational effectiveness. The focus of this work is often around helping individuals manage through change that is happening in their organizational unit – whether implementing a new technology, developing a new marketing plan, expanding, or reducing staff. Individuals and their departments collectively require a set of personal and organizational capabilities. In working with these leaders and their organizations, the areas they are often seeking to develop, such as change management, resilience, peripheral thinking, or systems thinking, are the same adaptive capabilities that are required for success in a VUCA environment.

As coaches, we have a unique opportunity to help prepare our clients for success in this new world. There are a number of adaptive responses that we can help guide our clients to develop. Developing a sense of perspective, for example, can help our clients to gauge their response to difficult circumstances, rather than react in unproductive ways. Another capability we can help develop is insight. Insight provides more or better information to draw on and helps clients make better decisions and choices when faced with challenging circumstances.

In some ways, VUCA is not a new threat or opportunity; it is the new normal, the way it is now. We are well served to operate every day with a set of capabilities that empowers us to re-invest, re-design, and re-invent ourselves almost in the moment. It is an exciting time to be in the business of coaching others to be more successful in their daily lives and work.

> *"We are well served to operate every day with a set of capabilities that empowers us to re-invest, re-design, and re-invent ourselves almost in the moment."*

COACHING FOR VUCA ACUMEN

Bob Johansen, author of *Leaders Make the Future: Ten New Leadership Skills for an Uncertain World* and a distinguished fellow at the Institute for the Future, came up with an opposing archetype to counter Volatility, Uncertainty, Complexity, and Ambiguity. He notes that skills in Vision, Understanding, Clarity, and Agility can be applied to more effectively manage in a VUCA environment.

As coaches, we can use these as a blueprint for guiding our clients toward creating vision, building understanding, seeking clarity, and acting with agility.

For the purpose of this chapter, I am taking the perspective of providing coaching services to leaders, leaders of people and organizations of any variety, whether for profit or not-for-profit. The client leaders who best benefit from coaching for VUCA acumen are those who have responsibility for others in the organization and largely get work done through others.

COACHING FOR VISION

Volatility in our environment, such as an economic downturn, overnight competition, or even natural disaster, can be countered with Vision. Some organizations are in the business of managing volatility, such as an insurance company skilled at planning for and calculating the probability of future disasters and skilled at delivering relief in disastrous circumstances. Likewise, our leader clients can better prepare to manage through turbulent times by having a plan and direction in place now. By anticipating possible future scenarios, they can better address environmental changes such as economic downturns or new competition in their markets (when they come.... and they will come).

Professor Paul Shoemaker of The Wharton School wrote a book about this phenomenon of peripheral vision. He says that most organizational leaders are completely surprised by environmental events, such as the emergence of new competition or changes in consumer patterns, despite warning signs that appear in the periphery of the business' view. Developing peripheral vision is critical to forming a strategic vision that will still be relevant in one, three, or five years down the road.

Unless your client is at the top of the organization, others typically set the vision and direction for the work they do. Most leaders are responsible for bringing the corporate vision, goals, and strategies down to the next level.

> *"Ask your client how they share their understanding of the vision, goals, and strategies with their direct team."*

When coaching a leader-client to build visioning skills, consider these processes:
- ✓ It is important to understand the company direction and what is important for success. This will empower your client to align her own thinking toward the bigger picture. Ask your client for their organization's mission statement, vision, goals, and strategies. If your client was not involved in the development of the vision, suggest that they talk with others who were involved to gain their understanding.
- ✓ Ask your client how they share their understanding of the vision, goals, and strategies with their direct team. Explore providing the team with background information so the direction makes sense to them. It is helpful for others to

know the strategic options discussed and the context in which decisions were made so they will have a richer understanding of the direction chosen. By having your client create this understanding in others they are more likely to buy into and support the vision.
- ✓ Challenge your client to explore approaches for discussing their expectations with the group, including the approach they will take to build the vision, goals, and strategies for their part of the organization. It helps to define the process that they will use so that they are prepared when engaging the team in the work.
- ✓ Once your client has the vision, goals, and strategies for the business unit or team, ask them to review them against the criteria the team is using to ensure accomplishment of the corporate and business unit goals. Challenge them to look for alignment. Where alignment is lacking, the client may determine whether there is good reason for it. If not, the client can adjust the strategy to ensure it supports the strategic direction of the company.

If your client already has goals and strategies, consider this process:
- ✓ Review the team or business goals and strategies against the corporate or business unit goals and strategies. Ask your client to describe areas of alignment. Where are the differences? What do they want to change? What can remain?

- ✓ Your client may want to discuss any lack of alignment with peers, explain their rationale, and see if their peers are willing to support it. Most likely your client will want others' support in some way, so it is a good idea to for the client to gain their agreement ahead of time.
- ✓ Ask the client how they monitor the team's work for consistency with the plan and the priorities that they have set on an ongoing basis. Explore their business strategy as a living document and use it to focus and guide their actions, and the actions of the team.

COACHING FOR UNDERSTANDING

Uncertainty can be countered with understanding. "Seek first to understand, then to be understood." This famous quote by Steven Covey certainly resonates here. Developing understanding requires that a leader-client stop, look, and listen to others inside and outside their immediate organization. Developing understanding involves communicating with all levels of employees in their organization. This is supported by developing and demonstrating teamwork and collaboration skills.

In an environment of open communication, people feel reasonably comfortable sharing information, whether it is positive or negative. When coaching a leader-client to create understanding, use these processes:

- ✓ Ask your client about the value of seeking the opinions of others before they make a decision, so that they are open to others' influence.   If your client asks for input after they have already made a decision, they may not be as willing to listen to other ideas and opinions, especially if they contradict the decision your client has set in their own mind.
- ✓ When asking people for their opinions, it is important to back up one's words with action.   Ask your client for their plan to listen intently and thank people for their ideas, take their ideas seriously, and consider ways to incorporate other's ideas when appropriate.   Most importantly, ask your client how they will give others credit for the ideas they contributed.
- ✓ We all benefit when we value other's views.   When your client hears an idea that does not seem to make sense, ask them about taking some time to consider it.   Although this approach may seem uncomfortable, over time your client will benefit from having access to a wider range of information and ideas.
- ✓ It can be difficult to guard against showing frustration with people who express contrary views to our own.   Doing so, even in subtle ways, will inhibit other from offering their views in the future.   When your client is faced with these situations, rather than viewing dissension, differences of opinion, or disagreement as obstacles, ask them how they will set themself up to think of them as opportunities for further exploration.

- ✓ It is important to give people options for expressing their views. For example, some people may not feel comfortable expressing themselves face-to-face or in a public setting. Ask your client how they will ask people to convey their ideas and opinions in a way that is comfortable for them.
- ✓ Monitoring our reactions to situations in which people from different levels, functions, or cultures express contrary views supports gaining insights for the long term. How does your client respond? Is their response effectively supporting their long-term results? Is it fair to the person expressing their view? Challenge your client to decide how to monitor their reactions in these situations.

> *"Challenge your client to decide how to monitor their reactions in these situations."*

When you listen intently, it shows that you are interested in another person's ideas. It also signals a willingness to learn from that person, and to work together cooperatively. Consider the following processes during your coaching sessions:

- ✓ Perhaps one of the most difficult things we face in conversation is to accept silence as part of it. Even though it may be uncomfortable, ask you client how they will handle silence and what the impact is on the circumstances. Ask them about using the time to think and reflect about what the person said.

✓ Support your client to focus on the content of the conversations they have with others in the workplace through questions: What is the main idea the person is trying to convey? What are the facts? Your client may want to ask some questions that explore the background so that they can better understand the other person's viewpoint. They may also want to ask clarifying questions. This is especially useful when listening to people who include a lot of detail in their messages.
✓ When coaching your client ask them to think about how much time they spend talking versus listening during a typical conversation at work. Ask them the benefit of giving other people a chance to talk. Ask what will happen if they spend at least half of their time listening.
✓ Ask your client about nonverbal actions that indicate they are listening and receptive to what is being said. These include facing the other person, using eye contact, and nodding.

COACHING FOR CLARITY

Complexity can be countered with clarity. Gaining clarity requires a leader to sift through the chaos of complex situations and events, and focus on what matters most. Gaining clarity is a very deliberative process of tuning out the noise that may surround a situation and tuning into the truth in order to make better, more informed business decisions.

Many people become uncomfortable when they do not know exactly what is expected of them, or when there is no clear leader or structure. When coaching a client to work productively in these situations, consider providing the following guidance:

- ✓ Ask your client how they will look for the possibilities in an ambiguous situation. For example, your client might have an opportunity to take on a new or more responsibility. In those situations, ask about new approaches or new ideas because in ambiguous situations, there is unlikely a precedent on how to handle the situation.

- ✓ Ask the client about seeking opportunities to work in unstructured situations, such as informal problem-solving groups, brainstorming sessions, or task forces. These can provide opportunities to practice being more flexible.

- ✓ Explore how the client can use their expertise and experience to make an educated guess about unknown factors. Also, ask them which more experienced colleagues they want to talk with about the situation. Your client may find that a situation is clearer than it first appears.

- ✓ Ask your client how they will stay productive if they feel a lack of clarity. Ask them how they will move past ambiguity. Ask the client how they will maintain focus on the areas in which they can move forward, set some goals, and take action.

✓ Remember that things change over time. Ask your client how they will keep learning, ask questions, and be persistent.

> *"Ask the client about seeking opportunities to work in unstructured situations..."*

I have found that during annual employee opinion surveys, many organizations learn that employees are completely unsure of how their work contributes to the overall organizational strategy. Employees don't have that line of sight so their work may feel meaningless or unimportant. In order for an organization to succeed during VUCA times, it is even more important that *everyone* in the organization has clarity of purpose in their job and fully understands how their individual contribution adds value to the broader strategy and purpose of the organization. Tying individual goals and tasks to the team's and the organization's objectives can help employees see the broader purpose for their work. When coaching a leader-client to provide clarity in these situations, use these processes:

✓ When your client is communicating their team's vision and mission, ask them how they will use specific, real-life examples to make the vision and mission clear and captivating to others. Ask how exactly they will link individual's work to the overall objectives of the organization.

- ✓ When setting new objectives, ask the client how they will engage their employees with how the work will support the goals of the group and the organization as a whole. For example, the client can discuss with their employees how the outcome will affect profitability, improve customer satisfaction, or drive new business.
- ✓ Ask your client how they let their team members know that they are available to discuss the purpose and mission of their work. Sometimes people prefer to meet one-on-one to talk about issues like this, so they can ask questions without worrying about how the group will view them.
- ✓ Ask your client how they discuss with their team how the group is measuring up against the overall objectives of the company. For example, if one of the organization's goals is customer responsiveness, ask your client how feedback they have received from customers and others about the group's responsiveness is handled.
- ✓ Realize that clarifying the purpose and mission of any team's work is a process, not an event. Ask your client how they will continue to communicate with and update others on the team's progress against their goals and keep people informed of changes as they occur.

> *"Coaching for agility may be the most challenging Because it requires that the client approach a situation in ways that are outside their comfort-zone."*

COACHING FOR AGILITY

Finally, ambiguity can be countered with agility. Agility requires that we move swiftly in our response to act and apply solutions.

A change jolts people who have settled into comfortable habits and patterns, and may make them feel ill-at-ease. Change also compels people to learn new skills, continually push beyond their comfort zones, and approach situations in fresh ways. Coaching for agility may be the most challenging because it requires that the client approach a situation in ways that are outside their comfort-zone. Consider the following methods:

- ✓ Discuss with your client how processes, procedures, and other methods at work frequently change. Most organizations want to do things better and faster; and this means that everyone's work will be affected at times.
- ✓ When your client first encounters a new way of doing something, explore it so that they pause and reflect on the change. Ask the client how much time they want to give the new approach before they express a reaction. Ask how they will consider the potential benefits of the new approach, and how to potentially adopt it.
- ✓ Ask your client options for understanding the change, what is driving it, and what it will do for their team and the larger organization. For example, attend all meetings and training sessions, or discuss the new approach with their colleagues

and manager. As your client better understands the reasoning behind new ways of doing things, they will increase their own effectiveness at adapting to them.

- ✓ Ask your client about how they are perceived as a role model. Although it may be challenging to adapt to different ways of doing things, encouraging others to adapt can make it easier. Helping others make the transition is as important as making it yourself.

- ✓ Ask your client how they will ensure they think positively. If the client considers change as a challenge or opportunity to think creatively, they can begin to see that a new way of doing things is a chance to improve, and there is generally room for improvement.

- ✓ Ask your client about possible changes on the horizon. A key part of being versatile is seeing what is coming around the corner and preparing for it.

- ✓ Ask the client about their own motivations and challenges with adapting to change. For example, is it because they are comfortable with routine, or because the original approach was the client's idea and they do not want to give that up? Identifying internal motivations and owning up to them is an important step to freeing oneself up to be more open to the change.

- ✓ If your client says "that's the way it has always been done" ask them for reasons to stay with that approach and for reasons to change the approach. The best solutions answer the demand or the challenge, and new challenges often require new solutions.

Because uncertainty is present, every decision involves an element of risk. The ability to recognize and take calculated risks is a skill required of all managers. As your client works on challenges, explore the following:

- ✓ What is their analysis of their plans and implementation process? What are the points at which the process could be halted – the "go/no go" decision points? How will the client inform others of these points so they will not be surprised if the client decides to discontinue the process.

- ✓ Ask your client to write down each alternative and its associated risks and benefits. Then ask them how they will choose to provide the greatest benefit with an awareness for balancing some risk. Ask them how they will manage the risk, anticipate problems, plan for contingencies, and deal with challenges as they arise.

- ✓ People may become so uncomfortable about the possible consequences of a risky decision that they avoid taking risks altogether. Ask your client the worst thing that could happen as a result of this decision. Ask how much impact this "worst thing" could have personally, on the organization, or on the work. Ask the client to determine what they could do if the worst-case scenario occurred. By putting a 'plan B' in place, a contingency plan, then your client can free them self to take a chance on a more risky and potentially rewarding course of action.

Parting Thoughts

If we embrace change as a constant present factor, we can better set ourselves up for success with whatever the world brings. In some ways the best coaching we can provide for our leader clients and others is to simply create the awareness for keeping an open mind. By approaching each day and each situation we face with a flexible world-view, we empower ourselves to see the different possibilities and opportunities amidst the volatility, uncertainty, complexity, and ambiguity in our lives with vision, understanding, clarity, and agility.

> *"The ability to recognize and take calculated risks is a skill required of all managers."*

Maria Van Parys is an executive in human resources with global experience in all functions. She is a subject matter expert in leadership, talent management, and organization development. Maria is recognized for rapid delivery of high quality HR programs and business solutions.

Maria has led all corporate HR functions including talent acquisition, learning and development, talent management, diversity and inclusion, compensation and benefits, HRIS, and HR Operations. She's worked for a diverse set of Boston-based companies in insurance and financial services, software development, software consulting, and medical devices. She's led several integrations, mergers, and acquisitions and helped build a global HR Business Partner organization.

Maria has delivered leadership training programs across the U.S., Europe, Asia, India, and the Middle East.

Maria holds a Bachelor's degree from Providence College and a Master's in Organizational Learning from Suffolk University. She is certified as a Senior Professional in Human Resources (SPHR) and as a Certified Professional Coach (CPC).

http://www.linkedin.com/pub/maria-van-parys/2/1ab/167

FINDING YOUR IDEAL CLIENT
by Nozomi Morgan

Are you loving being a coach and struggling to get clients? Do you have clients that are vague, undecided, or not fully committed? Are you hesitant to market yourself and your business? Are you afraid of putting yourself out there? Are these roadblocks preventing you from being a successful coach? These roadblocks are symptoms of your own fear. The fear of being rejected, fear of not getting responses, fear of hearing no, fear of thinking I am not good enough, and the fear of failing. Are these fears holding you back from being a successful coach and a business owner? I know many coaches that struggle with these symptoms. I am also guilty of many of these symptoms. It took me a full year after I launched my business to send out an email to my long list of contacts to tell them that I started my coaching business. I made every excuse in the book to not announce to the world about my new endeavor. I worried about many things: I don't have a logo. I don't have a tag line. I don't have enough experience as a coach. I'm not sure who my target audience is. My website doesn't look professional enough. What if a prospect contacts me and doesn't like me? What if they think my services are too expensive? What if the client is not satisfied with my coaching? What if, what if, what if! I could go on forever.

"What if, what if, what if!"

My fear was holding me back and not allowing me to shine. What is ironic is that I am a marketing expert. My whole corporate career was in marketing. In my corporate days, when I worked with clients I had crystal clear clarity in what they should do to achieve their business goals. I never thought I would lose objectivity with my own business. It's so much easier to make rational decisions when you don't have emotional attachments to them. I struggled with who my ideal clients were and what services I would offer. I wanted to serve everyone that I possibly could and do it all! I wanted to do coaching, training, speaking, writing and anything that I could get my hands on all at once. Then I realized I was spreading myself too thin and had completely lost objectivity. I wasn't making decisions logically. I wasn't analyzing myself or my business. I was doing things from the fear of missing out. What if I don't target this group and miss out potential revenue? What if I limit my services and miss out on prospects that wanted something else? I couldn't focus on a niche. I was afraid to let go.

It's natural to feel scared and uncomfortable when you dive into something new. There is added pressure when you are a full time coach and all of your income relies on your business. If you are reading this there is no doubt that you are committed and you want to be a successful coach and business owner. My purpose for writing this chapter is to put an end to this struggle. I will share keys to make your coaching business successful by focusing on marketing, defining your ideal client and how to communicate with them.

WHAT MAKES A BUSINESS SUCCESSFUL?

"Good news: Marketing is simple."

The key to any successful business is marketing. Did you get a gag reflection when you heard the M word? Some people might automatically shut down when they hear the word marketing. Good news: Marketing is simple. I want to clear up one big misconception of marketing: marketing is not selling. When you do marketing right, you do not have to sell. Clients will want your product and service because they realize the value and how it will benefit them. We are exposed to marketing all the time. We live and breathe through marketing from the most obvious to the more discrete. Are you one of those people who say you have never done marketing before? I have to call you out on that one. I don't know you; I am confident that you have done marketing. You had your first marketing campaign before you knew it. When you were a child did you ever ask your parents to buy a certain toy that you just had to have? Did you tell them that it's a good idea to get the toy because it enhances your learning and you can play with it with siblings or you can easily hand them down and that is why it makes perfect sense to buy it for you? Did you plan the perfect moment to tell them? That's marketing! Even as a child, you knew what your parent was looking for in a toy and what would make them want to buy it for you. You learned from observing your parents, gathering data points from analyzing their shopping behavior, listening to their conversations, and interacting with them. You naturally figured out who to talk to, when to bring it up, how to persuade them, and what to tell them. No one taught you what to do; you naturally figured it out because you wanted to get the toy. Marketing is not just for so-called marketers. Talking to someone while you are standing in the line at the grocery store about your business is also marketing. It is a very simple concept that everyone naturally does, yet finds a way to make it complicated by losing focus.

> *"Marketing for coaches is serving your ideal clients by making your product and service available..."*

Let me give you my definition of marketing for coaches: Marketing for coaches is serving your ideal clients by making your product and service available to your ideal client through an adequate contact point and timing. Marketing is about providing your product and service to people who would benefit from them. In other words, you are not serving your client if you don't make your service noticeable or available. Marketing is different from selling. Marketing is providing the right product and service to the right person. As the business owner you are responsible to know who is the right person, or as I like to say, the ideal client.

AN IDEAL CLIENT

An ideal client is a client with which you, as a coach, can create the ultimate win-win coaching relationship. You make a positive impact on your client. The client gets the outcome that they wanted and is satisfied and happy. When the client is happy the coach is happy. On top of that, you, the coach, enjoy working with the client. Most importantly though, your ideal client understands the worth of working with you and pays you with open arms. Your ideal client will spread the word about you to his or her network. This happy relationship is the ultimate win-win relationship that you can get when you are working with your ideal client. Imagine how much fun and reward there is working with such amazing clients! It will be fabulous when all your coaching relationships are like this. I hear you asking, "How do I find such wonderful clients?"

When I talk about marketing, I like to use the analogy of dating. I assume that everyone that is reading this has experienced dating at least once and probably more. If you have any experience in dating, then you are already an expert marketer. Dating naturally engages you in the activity of marketing. It requires a lot of sophisticated marketing skills. Think of the date you want to get as your ideal client. How would you get your date to notice you, get interested in you, and then say yes to going out with you? Where would you start? The answer is simple. Start with knowing yourself.

You want to have a clear understanding of who you are, the reasons you are a coach, what your values are, what makes you unique, and what makes you happy. It's very important that you write everything down and get your thoughts on to paper. This will help you organize your thoughts and also look at them objectively. With a sheet of paper take your time and write the answers to the questions below.

TEN CLARITY QUESTIONS TO KNOW YOURSELF DEEPER

1. For what reasons did I become a coach?
2. What is my vision as a coach?
3. What is my mission as a coach?
4. What services do I offer?
5. What three things are most important to me?
6. What three values do I stay true to?
7. How am I unique?
8. What three to five things as a coach do I do well?
9. What are three to five things as a coach that I will not tolerate?
10. What are three to five things that make me happy?

I am sharing my answers to give you an idea for starting. This is an ongoing process and you will be revisiting this over and over again. Just go through the questions and start writing your thoughts down. Sleep on it, think about it, and write more. As you work with more and more clients, your thoughts will evolve.

The point is to start exploring your thoughts on paper and obtaining clarity.

Here are my answers as an example:

1. For what reasons did I become a coach?

I became a coach because I wanted to positively impact other people's lives. I want to help people to become the person they want to be and live the life they want. I want to help people to be happy, be on the path of authentic success, and shine.

2. What is my vision as a coach?

I want people to shine and make this world a brighter place.

3. What is my mission as a coach?

I coach experienced international professionals to help them find their authentic success and live their best life.

4. What services do I offer?

I offer one-on-one and group coaching. I train and speak on leadership, professional development, personal branding, and cross cultural communication at seminars and workshops.

5. What three things are most important to me?

Family, health and adding value to society

6. What three values can I not compromise?

Honesty, respect and gratitude

7. How am I unique?

I have a rich international background and speak English and Japanese fluently. I lived and studied in four countries and have traveled to more than thirty countries. My background is in advertising and marketing with industry leaders. I have worked in both Japan and the U.S., and have experienced the challenges that professionals go through in their career and life in both countries. I currently live in Atlanta, Georgia. I have the flexibility to travel to Japan.

8. What three to five things as a coach do I do well?

Life and career strategy, productivity, confidence, motivation, cross cultural awareness, and marketing

9. What are three to five things as a coach that I will not tolerate?

Disrespect, tardiness, unprofessionalism, and dishonesty

10. What are three to five things that make me happy?

When people around me are happy
When I'm spending quiet time with people and things I love
When I wake up in the morning and face the new day

Many dating experts tell you to make a list of what you want in your future mate. They have a point. How can you find a soul mate if you don't know what you want in your soul mate? It is crucial in dating and also in business to know what you want. I once made a list about a guy, too. The list goes like this. I want to be with someone who: (1) Enjoys food; (2) Is open minded and accepts different cultures; (3) Has a good education; (4) Loves animals; (5) Is well-traveled; (6) Enjoys cooking; (7) Appreciates nice and beautiful things; (8) Has a good career; (9) Is in a good relationship with his family; and (10) Will always love me as I am. This list was actually more helpful than I ever imagined. I was able to say no to dates that were not worth my time without fearing that I might be missing out, while preventing me from wasting my time and energy on dates that had no future. After I made this list, I met a very nice guy who passed nine out of ten on the list. The only one that he didn't check was number five, which was not a deal-breaker. It's easy to get distracted by shiny things and smooth talks. The old me might have overlooked how special he was without this list. The list really worked for me. That guy is now my husband! Defining your ideal client calls for more specifics. The next set of clarity questions are put together to help you extract what kind of person you want to work with and equally importantly with whom you do NOT want to work. On another sheet of paper write the answers to the five questions below.

FIVE CLARITY QUESTIONS TO KNOW WITH WHOM YOU WANT TO WORK

1. Who do I most want to work with? List ten words that describe who you most want to work with.

2. Who do I know I could help?
3. What makes me want to work with them?
4. What are the basic demographics of my ideal client?
    a. Gender?
    b. Age?
    c. Marital Status?
    d. Nationality/Ethnicity?
    e. Language?
    f. Children? How many?
    g. Work?
    h. Annual household income?
    i. Spirituality/Religion?
    j. Where does he/she live (geographically)?
    k. Home/condo/apartment/etc?
    l. Pets?
    m. Lifestyle/hobbies?
    n. Family/siblings?
    o. What else?
5. Who do I absolutely NOT want to work with? List five attributes that describe who you do not want to work with.

Here are my answers as an example:

1. Who do I most want to work with? List ten words that describe with whom you most want to work.
Motivated, hard worker, respectful, smart, appreciative, positive, open, ready for change, mindful, and on-time

2. Who do I know I could help?
Someone who is humble and wants to find their authentic career and life.

3. What makes me want to work with them?
I want to work with my ideal client because I know how it feels to be lost and not satisfied with a career and life. I had a good career even though I was not happy. For ten years or so, I was looking for a career and life that I would be passionate about. Once my ideal client has clarity, they will be able to do so much more and be a force of greater good.

4. What are the basic demographics of my ideal client?
    a. Gender? Male and female
    b. Age? 30+
    c. Marital Status? Single or married
    d. Nationality/Ethnicity? Japanese and non-Japanese
    e. Language? English and Japanese
    f. Children? How many? None to a few
    g. Work? Professionals working for a company or have their own business
    h. Annual household income? $80,000 +
    i. Spirituality/Religion? Any
    k. Where does he/she live? Japan or North America
    l. Home/condo/apartment/etc? Home, condo or apartment
    m. Pets? Cat and/or dog or none

n. Lifestyle/hobbies? Healthy lifestyle, yoga, running, reading

o. Family/siblings? Have a relationship with their mother, father, and siblings

p. What else? Has international background, self-motivated, frequently reads personal development books or attends seminars

5. Who do I absolutely NOT want to work with? List five attributes that describe who you do not want to work with.
Someone who does not value my time, who is not ready to be coached, or who is not open to new perspectives and changes

Now you have written down with whom you do and do not want to work. You know who your ideal client is and you can pick them out of a crowd. When some people arrive at this point, they suddenly get scared. They think that their ideal target is too narrow. They fear that they are missing out on opportunities by eliminating the people who might be interested in their service. The good news is that you are not alone. It is natural to feel this way. I hear many people saying, "Isn't a bigger target easier to hit?" If you were in archery competition, I would say, "Yes, you are right." Wise marketers think differently. The smaller the target the better! When your target is broad, the message will become vague. When the

"The smaller the target the better!"

message is vague, the target does not feel that you are talking to them. It would be too general. Think of how prospects decide on a coach. After performing all the due diligence, ultimately they will choose the coach they feel they can connect with and trust.

How do you make that connection? For example, let's get back to the dating analogy. Imagine you are sixteen years old again and wanting to date the girl or boy who sits in front of you in your English class. You want to know everything about them. What music do they listen to? What is their favorite clothing brand? What do they like or dislike eating? Where do they go after school? Which TV programs do they watch? What book are they reading now? What snack are they obsessed with now? Which college are they considering? You want to know everything about them so you can start a conversation with them and connect with them. Instead of asking them out the minute you meet, you wait until you create that connection and build trust... Then you know the time is right to ask them to go out with you.

WHAT DO YOU COMMUNICATE?

After identifying your ideal client, determine how to effectively communicate with your ideal client. In order to get their attention and grab their heart, you will want to know everything about your ideal client. In addition to the basic demographic information that is on the surface, you want to dig deep and understand what they really want and need. Your goal is to become the subject matter expert on your ideal client. This is the reason a smart marketer knows the smaller target yields favorable results. When you define a focused clear target, your message becomes clearer and resonates with your ideal client. Your client will instantly feel that you understand them and you know them well. Take out another sheet of paper and write the answers to the following ten questions.

TEN QUESTIONS TO CLARIFY YOUR IDEAL CLIENT'S WANTS

1. What are the five results that my ideal client wants?
2. What are the five fears that prevent them from achieving their wants?
3. What are the three biggest challenges my ideal client has?
4. How do these challenges appear in the ideal client's life?
5. What are the three mistakes my ideal client is making?
6. What are the mistakes my ideal client is making while thinking they are doing it right?
7. What are the things my ideal client has no idea how/what to do?
8. What is the one thing that my ideal client does not want anyone to know about them?
9. What is the one thing that my ideal client does not want to admit to themselves?

10. What is the one thing that will make my ideal client happy?

Here are my answers as an example:
1. What are the five results that my ideal client wants?
The ideal client wants clarity in knowing where their life and career are heading. They want to figure out what they really want to do. They want to know how to better utilize their strengths and talents. They want to know how to live a happy and successful life. They want to feel more confident in themselves.

2. What are the five fears that prevent them from achieving their wants?
They are afraid to fail. They are afraid to change. They are afraid that people won't accept what they want to do. They are afraid they might not be paid as much as they are now. They are afraid to do it and to realize what they have is better.

3. What are the three biggest challenges my ideal client has?
To overcome their fear of change and be open to new perspectives; to schedule time for themselves in a busy life; to step out of their comfort zones

4. How do these challenges appear in the ideal client's life?
They put off doing anything about their current situation and do nothing.

5. What are the three mistakes my ideal client is making?
Collecting knowledge on how to change their lives without taking actions. Trying to feel satisfied and filling the hole in their heart by spending time with their friends or doing fun things, without taking any new action. Thinking that if they work harder or if they wait just a little bit longer things will get better.

6. What are the mistakes my ideal client is making while thinking they are doing it right?
They believe that working hard and spending long hours at work will change the situation. Talking to friends and mentors, and not working with an expert that can really help them.
They try to solve everything by themselves.

7. What are the things my ideal client has no idea how/what to do?
They have no idea how to change the situation now. They have no idea how to ask for help.

8. What is the one thing that my ideal client does not want anyone to know about them?
That they have no clue what to do now.

9. What is the one thing that my ideal client does not want to admit to themselves?
That they are afraid to change and fail.

10. What is the one thing that will make my ideal client happy?

Knowing that they are on the right path.

How do you feel now? What thoughts came to your mind? The clarity question exercises throughout this chapter become the foundation of your marketing. Marketing is communicating to your ideal client at relevant touch points with relevant information to help them make the right decision. Great marketing helps your ideal client to easily make decisions.

> *"Marketing is communicating to your ideal client at relevant touch points with relevant information to help them make the right decision. Great marketing helps your ideal client to easily make decisions."*

In order to be excellent at marketing you and your business, there is one simple thing I want you to take away from this chapter: The key to your success as a coach comes from you. Knowing who you are and who you want to work with are the fundamentals of your marketing and business. Be honest with yourself and find that ideal client soul mate who values you for who you are and what you offer. When you come across someone that is not a good fit for you, refer that prospect to a fellow coach. It's more likely they will get better results and higher satisfaction. Your fellow coach will appreciate your gesture and might refer to you when they come across a prospect that is a better fit with you. You will be happy that you did the right thing for the prospect and yourself. You are being client-centered and thoughtful by referring the prospect to another coach that can better serve the prospect. At the end, this will make you, the prospects, and the other coaches all happy. Revisit and assess the profile of your ideal client every three to six months. As I work with more clients and gain clarity on my message and how to operate my business, I have a clearer focus on who my ideal client is. As you and your business grow, the ideal client profile will evolve and you will too.

Nozomi Morgan is President and Founder of Michiki Morgan Worldwide LLC. Known for her radiant smile, Nozomi is a Certified Master Coach who works with international professionals helping them become positive geniuses living the fulfilling life they want and finding their authentic success in careers. She coaches, speaks, and trains in English and Japanese on professional development, leadership, personal branding, and cross cultural business communication.

Clients benefit from Nozomi's global background, optimism, and 15 years of corporate marketing. Her experience includes industry-leading clients in the automotive, consumer packaging, fashion, entertainment, IT, lifestyle, finance, and airline sectors.

Nozomi is a world citizen. Born and raised in Japan, she values integrity, professionalism, and respect, all tenets of her deeply ingrained heritage. She has worked in Japan and the US, studied in four countries, lived in eight cities, and traveled to more than 30 countries. She continues to expand her world physically and intellectually while embracing the challenges.

Nozomi lives in the US and frequently travels to Tokyo. She is currently Director of Professional Development at the National Association of Asian American Professionals Atlanta Chapter.

www.NozomiMorgan.com

How to Increase Sales: A Coach's Perspective
by Jina Fernandez

When I first became a retail banker in the late 1980's, everyone working in the branch had a very specific duty. We had new account representatives who primarily focused on opening new accounts, customer service representatives and tellers who focused on efficiency and accuracy in meeting the customer's stated need, and yes, we even still had loan officers in the local branch to handle all things related to lending. To accommodate all of these specialized functions, the branch employed approximately 15-20 employees. Even the pace was different. We opened our doors at 9:00 am and served the customers who walked in until we closed the doors at 4:00 pm. Tellers did not have sales goals and the moderate sales goals of the new account representatives were often easily met by the foot traffic that walked through the door.

Fast forward to where we are today, and I believe most of us agree that our local bank branches look a lot different. Today's branches run on fewer employees who are trained to wear many hats, and it is often the same banker who is your new account representative, customer service representative, and loan specialist. The sales environment has also changed. With the expansion of technology and fewer customers choosing to bank in person, many retail bankers must be proactive to meet challenging sales goals, and every banker in the branch plays a role in uncovering sales opportunities.

Of course this change did not happen overnight. The migration from a reactive service environment to a proactive sales environment while still maintaining high levels of customer satisfaction required skill enhancement and continuous focus. So how did we accomplish the change? Supported by strong leadership and a shared vision for what our bank could become, a small group of us became coaches.

As a coach, my primary assignment was to assist retail bankers in enhancing their sales skills. I'm a firm believer in needs-based selling, so I designed much of my early coaching around creating a shift in thinking from selling to serving. This change in mindset was important because it allowed bankers to draw on something familiar as we transitioned from an organization primarily based on service to one equally focused on sales results. It also required that they sharpened their sales skills around asking questions, listening for clues about what the client really wanted, and matching that with the right products. Instinctively, I knew that this approach led to stronger customer relationships and long term satisfaction. Helping service-oriented bankers see that same perspective helped them sell through service.

I believe in the power of coaching and have seen how it can increase performance across a number of situations. Through a combination of observation, coaching, strategizing sessions, and sharing our expertise, sales productivity began to increase in the branches. So I was curious if others experienced the same results. A quick Internet search uncovered a number of studies touting the high return on coaching services. In the case of sales professionals, working with a coach can be especially impactful. The top three reasons I will explore in this chapter include:

- Modeling the Behavior – As coaches, we apply certain competencies that also translate to effective sales skills, because in both cases, our success is dependent on strong relationships. Where our coaching skills overlap with sales skills, we become a model for our coachees. As we apply active listening or powerful questioning in a coaching session, our coachees experience what it feels like to be on the receiving end of these shared competencies. After they experience the connection of working with someone who is fully present with them, they can embrace these skills and emulate them in their sales process. I will spend much of the chapter exploring these competencies.

> *"As coaches, we apply certain competencies that also translate to effective sales skills."*

- A Strong Advocate – To use one of my mother's favorite expressions, "No man is an island." Sales professionals often work in independent environments where they have to be self-motivated, independent thinkers who determine their sales strategy, and ultimately depend on themselves to make it all happen. Having a sales coach gives these professionals a safe and supportive environment to stretch their skills, a sounding board to help them strategize around how to accomplish what they want, and a cheerleader who will pick them up when times are tough.

- Creating Accountability – There are a number of ways that coaches create accountability. As a competency, the International Coach Federation (ICF) defines it as the "ability to hold attention on what is important for the client, and to leave responsibility with the client to take action." In other words, we hold up our client's vision by reminding them what they are working towards, and then create awareness around how their actions are either in or out of integrity with their personal commitments. This dynamic occurs in one-on-one coaching and in group coaching.

MODELING THE BEHAVIOR: WHERE COACHING COMPETENCIES AND SALES SKILLS INTERSECT

As I completed my formal coach certification training and learned about the Core Competencies as defined by the International Coach Federation, ICF, I quickly recognized a parallel between the sales skills around which I coached and the coaching skills I use today. While not all coaching competencies translate to a sales interaction, many of them do.

> *"...a parallel between the sales skills ...and the coaching skills..."*

The ICF Core Competencies are as follows:
A. Setting the Foundation
    o Meeting Ethical Guidelines and Professional Standards
    o Establishing the Coaching Agreement
B. Co-Creating the Relationship
    o Establishing Trust and Intimacy
    o Coaching Presence
C. Communicating Effectively
    o Active Listening
    o Powerful Questioning
    o Direct Communication
D. Facilitating Learning and Results
    o Creating Awareness
    o Designing Actions
    o Planning and Goal Setting
    o Managing Progress and Accountability

These competencies are only the headlines. The full definitions are much more detailed with several sub-categories.

While the full definitions may not apply, one could argue that all of these competencies, at least in part, could apply to an effective sales process. For example, think about your last major purchase. What was your experience? Did your sales person take the time to discover what you wanted at that moment? Did he or she ask questions to clarify what you really sought and restate it in your language to ensure understanding? Did she listen to your concerns or give you the opportunity to think through your purchase decision? Did you feel he acted in your best interest by delivering solutions that met your requirements? Or, did you receive the opposite of all of these things? Perhaps your sales person focused on his agenda and not yours. If so, you may have felt like he would do anything to make the sale, resulting in your internal alarm sounding, "It's time to run."

So let's take a look at how these competencies apply to sales.

A. Setting the Foundation

Ethical Guidelines – Regardless of one's profession, working with someone who is ethical and professional is something we all seek. We all want to feel like our coaches, advisors, or sales professionals are working in our best interest. We want to know that when sensitive information is shared, our professionals will keep our information confidential. And we want to know our sales professionals will offer real solutions for our interests. Therefore, most professional industries, including the ICF, require that their members or licensed representatives follow a Code of Conduct or pre-determined set of ethical standards. Whether or not your industry requires it, following ethical guidelines builds credibility with clients and long-term relationships.

> *"...most professional industries, including the ICF, require that their members or licensed representatives follow a Code of Conduct or pre-determined set of ethical standards."*

Coaching Agreement – As coaches, our first step is to establish the coaching agreement. There are actually two parts to this step – the formal agreement that defines the logistics of the coaching relationship (where, when, and how often coach and client will meet, fees, what is and is not coaching, etc.) and the coaching agreement for each individual session where the client decides the topic. Skillful coaches will often spend time to truly understand what the coachee is asking for in their session. They'll ask questions to clarify the client's true objectives and then restate the objective to ensure understanding. While this process may sound simple, assisting the client in gaining clarity around what they really want may require a curious coach who asks defining questions, and it can sometimes be the most powerful part of the session. Once coach and coachee are clear of the objective, they will continue with the collaborative process of exploring possibilities to achieve it.

In a sales situation, this step of clearly defining the customer's objective is equally important. Last Christmas, my husband and I started the task of decorating the house. Filled with the holiday spirit and ready for a fun day of decorating, we pulled our pre-lit tree from the garage and started to put the pieces together. Our Christmas joy quickly faded as our pre-lit tree became a half-lit tree with a huge dark section in the middle. After assessing what we thought was the problem, we went in search of a fuse to hopefully restore light to the middle of our tree. Several stops later, we found the right fuse and returned home thinking we had solved the problem. Instead, we solved the wrong problem. After replacing the fuse, we still had a dark tree.

We talked with many helpful sales people that day as we went from store to store trying to find the right size fuse for our tree. Some helped us find the right aisle within the store. Some checked the back when the shelves were empty. Some even recommended other stores when they did not have the fuse we sought. None, however, asked a single question about the tree to determine if a fuse was the real problem. The outcome may have been the same; I do wonder how much better our experience would have been if someone took the time to ask questions that uncovered the real problem and then offered the right solution.

B. Co-Creating the Relationship

Establishing Trust and Intimacy – As coaches, our effectiveness depends on our ability to establish trust with our clients so they feel free to share openly. While there are tangible steps we can take, including a confidentiality clause in our agreements, most trust is established through the intangibles of our interaction, and it starts at the very beginning of our sessions. It comes from showing genuine concern for our clients and by providing honest feedback. The same is true for an effective sales professional. Before presenting any information about your products or services, take a moment to get to know your prospective clients and how you can best serve them. When you take the time to show genuine interest in them and to find out what is really important to them, you will earn your client's trust and find they are much more receptive to the solutions you offer later in the sales process.

Coaching Presence – Having a strong coaching presence ties directly to the previous competency of establishing trust and intimacy. When we are fully present, our clients can feel it. They will know when they have our full attention, and when they do not. In our fast-paced world of cell phones and tablets, we sometimes find it hard to disconnect from the outside world and give the person in front of us our full attention. I once saw a segment on a morning news show about a restaurant that asks its patrons to check in their cell phones before dinner. Some resist at first; they ultimately comply as it is a requirement to stay for dinner. Without the distractions of the outside world, patrons relax and enjoy rich conversation with their dinner partner. Better yet, they remember what it feels like to be fully present with the person before them, and they find the experience powerful. When we are fully present, we hear what is being said, what is not said, the emotion or energy behind the words, and we can respond at a much deeper level. These same perceptive skills can help sales professionals better understand their clients and their interests. In terms of sales, it may lead to an upgraded product, or uncover possible objections so they can address them in the negotiations. Whether it is in coaching or in sales, when we are fully present, our clients feel well-served and we build long-term relationships.

C. Communicating Effectively

Active Listening – Active listening is a critical competency for coaches and it has many parts. The ICF's summary definition for this competency is the "ability to focus completely on what the client is saying and is not saying, to understand the meaning of what is said in the context of the client's desires, and to support client self-expression." Active listening goes beyond hearing. It requires that we engage all our senses to fully understand the client's meaning. It is paying attention to the subtle changes in a client's expression when discussing certain topics, and hearing what gives them energy and what drains them. It is the ability to paraphrase or reiterate what the client has shared with us so we may ensure and demonstrate understanding. These rephrasing techniques can also be used to emphasize a point. Repeating what a client has said supports client self-expression and allows the client another opportunity to connect with a value or awareness that has just come to light. When we listen "in the context of the client's desires," we stay focused on their agenda. We are listening for the clues that require further exploration and will lead to the real discovery that will ultimately propel the client towards success. In a sales situation, deeply listening allows you to better serve your clients because you will discover their real interests and motivations for making a purchase. So often, the best clues come in the form of subtle comments shared in casual conversation, or in their expression as they react to the features of a product. When a sales professional is astute to these clues, they can explore further and identify how to best meet client expectations.

> *"(ICF)... ability to ask questions that reveal the information needed for maximum benefit to the coaching relationship and the client."*

Powerful Questioning – Powerful questioning is an effective tool for identifying what is not being said in the conversation and get to the heart of the matter. The ICF defines this competency as the "ability to ask questions that reveal the information needed for maximum benefit to the coaching relationship and the client." Notice the definition ends with "maximum benefit to...the client." These questions create awareness for both you and your prospective clients around the real motivation behind the purchasing decision. Knowing this information helps you tailor your presentation to satisfy the right interest with the right solution, resulting in a happier client.

Direct Communication – I suspect we have all experienced a conversation where the person sharing their story gives you every detail, including weather conditions and the clothes they wore on the day of their story. About half way into the conversation, the story-teller will pause and ask, "Where was I going with this?" and sadly, you can't answer, because you, too, have lost track of the point. In coaching and in sales, direct communication keeps the conversation moving and everyone engaged. It is the "ability to communicate effectively during coaching sessions, and to use language that has the greatest positive impact on the client." My favorite phrase in this ICF definition is "the greatest positive impact on the client." What is most beneficial for the client to hear? Is it reassurance? Is it another perspective? Once we identify the message, direct communication is about delivering that message succinctly and in the client's language so that he or she is receptive and can use the information in a positive way. In a sales situation, direct communication can be especially effective at the close as you restate the client's wants or objectives for their purchase, and then directly match how your product meets those interests.

Using clear and direct communication that matches their requirements with the features and benefits of your product will make it easier for clients to decide on their purchases.

D.   Facilitating Learning and Results

Creating Awareness – The ICF summary definition of creating awareness is the "ability to integrate and accurately evaluate multiple sources of information, and to make interpretations that help the client to gain awareness and thereby achieve agreed-upon results."   In a coaching environment, creating awareness is about the client's growth.   Using many of the competencies covered above, we help our coachees gain clarity, see another perspective, or recognize when their actions are not in alignment with their values.   This broader view fosters client growth and moves them towards their desired outcome.   In a sales situation, it may be helping clients gain clarity about what they really want. Or it might be about broadening their perspective around what your product can do for them.   Once you and the client have clearly identified what they want and how your product or service meets that requirement, you can ask the prospective client to move forward with their purchasing decision.

Designing Actions – Designing actions, in a coaching context, is also about client growth.   The ICF defines this competency as the "ability to create with the client opportunities for ongoing learning during coaching and in work/life situations and for taking new actions that will most effectively lead to agreed-upon coaching results." While the summary definition provided here translates less clearly to a sales situation, there are components in how we apply this competency that are also required in certain sales situations. For example, the detailed definition goes on to say that designing actions "helps the client to focus on and systematically explore specific concerns and opportunities that are central to agreed-upon coaching goals." If we replace "coaching goals" with "financial goals" at the end of that definition, it sounds like a competency a financial advisor might use when preparing a needs analysis and financial plan. Bottom line, it is about getting the client to take action to satisfy a want or to move forward towards their goals.

> *"Bottom line, it is about getting the client to take action to satisfy a want or to move forward towards their goals."*

Planning and Goal Setting – The ICF summary definition of planning and goal setting is the "ability to develop and maintain an effective coaching plan with the client." It is about strategizing with the client to obtain their desired results. In many professional sales situations, this due diligence is a necessary step to help clients achieve long-term goals. For example, licensed financial advisors determine suitability through analysis before selling securities products, and often times the analysis is done with a long-term goal in mind. In today's world of complex financial products, this step is designed to ensure the products offered are in alignment with the client's current financial situation and their future financial goals. Managing Progress and Accountability – The context of this competency is likely different in a coaching situation than in a sales situation. If we look at the broader meaning, there are aspects of this competency that apply. For example, if we take our beloved pets to the vet for anything other than their annual check-up, we get a call the next day to check on them. That unexpected higher level of service solidifies our relationship with our vet clinic because we know they care enough to check-in. Also, in the example of a mortgage or life insurance purchase, there are many steps to manage after the client applies and before the case closes. How a sales professional manages the process before, during, and after the sale can either make or break a long-term relationship with that client.

> *"How a sales professional manages the process before, during, and after the sale can either make or break a long-term relationship with that client."*

As coaches, we serve our clients by applying these competencies, and when the time is right, we ask them to move forward towards their goals. The best sales professionals apply similar competencies because they, too, seek to serve their clients by identifying and offering solutions that meet their clients' interests.

A Strong Advocate: Coaching Sales Professionals for Success

Recently I met with Jeff Reeter, Managing Partner of Northwestern Mutual's Texas Financial Group – Houston, Austin, San Antonio, where he shared his views on the importance of coaching for sales professionals. Jeff leads a dynamic group of financial sales professionals and he is co-founder of the coaching company, Total BEST (Balance, Excellence, Service, and Truth). With his experience in sales and in coaching, I felt he was the perfect person to share his insights on this subject.

When I asked him his thoughts about the reasons coaching is so important for sales professionals, he first responded with a sports analogy. He said, "Sales professionals are like athletes, and their client appointments are like game day. Just as an athlete has a coach to prepare for the game, a sales professional works with their coach to set the game plan, structure, and process to succeed." The analogy also fits when describing skill building. Much like a baseball coach helps a player adjust his swing, or learn a new pitch, a sales coach helps to build skills by applying the competencies outlined above. Sales coaches assume many of the same roles as our athletic counterparts, with one exception. Where athletic coaches set the direction for their teams, we co-create with our coachees in a collaborative environment. We explore possibilities, broaden perspective, and share observations. Ultimately, the coachee determines the best strategy to achieve the desired outcome. This distinction of who ultimately decides the strategy is an important one, because when the game is on the line, it is up to the coachee to own their actions, and we coaches must wait on the sidelines. Finally, much like a coach during a crucial locker room speech, we provide encouragement, celebrate successes, and hold the vision for our clients when they seek to find the strength to push through adversity.

> *"Imagine a bicycle where the front wheel is the sales process and the spokes are all of the steps and skills required to successfully complete a sale. Notice the front wheel includes everything sales related; at the same time, as a bicycle, it does not function without the back wheel. The crucial back wheel represents everything else that creates balance and stability in our lives – faith, family, health, etc. This back wheel provides balance and stability, and it is also the wheel that drives the bicycle forward."*

In our conversation, Jeff offered a second analogy that defines the importance of balance. Imagine a bicycle where the front wheel is the sales process and the spokes are all of the steps and skills required to successfully complete a sale. Notice the front wheel includes everything sales related; at the same time, as a bicycle, it does not function without the back wheel. The crucial back wheel represents everything else that creates balance and stability in our lives – faith, family, health, etc. This back wheel provides balance and stability, and it is also the wheel that drives the bicycle forward.

As coaches, we understand the importance of coaching the whole person. Much like in the analogy above, when the back wheel is off, the bicycle does not function. In a coaching relationship, we meet the coachee wherever they are in each coaching session, and address whatever issue is required to restore balance and to create maximum momentum.

CREATING ACCOUNTABILITY: THROUGH INDIVIDUAL AND GROUP COACHING

I cannot recall hearing anyone express a desire to live out of integrity with their values or commitments, and at the same time we live in a world where missed deadlines and broken promises are often a reality. When our actions are out of alignment with our values, it is rarely a result of a conscious desire to break our word. Instead, life happens, and we sometimes find ourselves reacting to the issues of the day instead of approaching the day with intention. Working with a coach helps clients clearly define their values and priorities, so they can live their lives with intention.

Accountability in the coaching sense is not the same as it is in sales management. A coach creates accountability by providing a safe space where clients can check in and report their progress, or lack of progress, towards stated commitments. When the client has made progress, we celebrate success and build on the momentum of the action steps already taken towards the client's goals. When a client misses a deadline, we listen openly for two important reasons. First, we are listening for clues about what is the real source behind the inaction so we can address the issue head-on. Second, we preserve a productive environment where the client remains open. We rely on our competencies, including direct communication, creating awareness, and designing actions, to identify the source that is holding the client back and help them move forward.

This dynamic of accountability can be powerful in a group coaching environment. I recently participated in a group led by a masterful group coach, Ginger Cockerham, MCC, CMC. While in Ginger's 12 Keys Mentoring program, I experienced accountability in a whole new way. I remember Ginger explaining during our first session that we would feel a change in momentum once the group "formed." And she was right. The structure of the sessions provided a time for each member to give an update on progress towards stated goals, and based on the energy in the calls, it seemed everyone wanted to come ready to deliver a good report. Even with these check-ins, the atmosphere always felt safe and supportive. As momentum began to build, member's commitment became two-fold. We wanted to give as much as we received, and our desire for success included success for ourselves and for the whole group.

A Coach's Perspective: How to Increase Sales

In summary, I believe in the power of coaching because I have experienced it personally and have seen the impact on those I have coached. Whether it is through modeling the behavior, being a strong advocate, or creating accountability, we create a safe collaborative space for our coachees to formulate their best game plan, and then support them through execution.

The most important gift we give our coachees is our presence – our complete attention to their agenda. We enhance that gift through our other competencies to create trust and build long-term relationships. As a sales professional, what better gift can you offer your clients than being present with them and serving their agenda?

I hope I have shared a few insights about how the best coaches and sales professionals lead with a servant's heart. It is where our processes overlap that we can achieve great success.

Jina Fernandez is a Certified Professional Coach with a passion for helping others succeed. An experienced retail banker, licenced insurance agent, and real estate investor, she understands that successful business begins with strong relationships. She brings that dedication to her coaching clients by providing a collaborative environment for growth.

Jina began coaching with retail bankers in 2001 to increase sales performance. She also mentored branch managers during the implementation of new sales processes, and facilitated strategic planning sessions for achieving revenue goals. She delivered training including customized workshops, one-on-one coaching, and mentoring. Jina then brought her expertise to insurance companies applying her strategic planning and coaching skills to help financial advisors and small business owners. With a personal desire to explore new things, Jina brought her business skills to real estate investing. She successfully restored a 55 year-old home and added modern conveniences for a profitable sale. While she found the transformation of the home rewarding, she missed the smiles and shared celebrations with coachees after achieving milestones. She returned to coaching to focus her efforts on creating pathways to higher performance.

She lives in Katy, TX with her husband Ray, a CPA and Certified Financial Planner.

Made in the USA
Columbia, SC
25 April 2018